GETTING TO THE HEART
OF YOUR MARRIAGE

GETTING TO THE HEART OF YOUR MARRIAGE

David A Holden

EDITOR AND CONCEPT DEVELOPMENT:
Vincent M. Newfield ❖ New Fields & Company ❖ www.newfieldscreativeservices.com

COVER DESIGN:
Jeremy Goldsborough ❖ ProChurch, Inc. ❖ www.prochurch.com

INTERIOR DESIGN:
Create Space ❖ www.createspace.com

First Printing

"*Getting to the Heart of Your Marriage* is a foundational book addressing the core issues within the marriage relationship. Strong marriages don't just happen! Learned negative relational patterns often lead couples away from one another and towards independence and isolation. *Getting to the Heart of Your Marriage* instead promotes oneness as Dave guides the reader through each core issue. Practical questions at the end of each chapter help apply what has been learned, promoting intimacy and strengthening the marriage relationship. I believe *Getting to the Heart of Your Marriage* is an essential resource for all marriages!!"

– Sherrie Drury
Bible Study Fellowship Teaching Leader

"*Getting to the Heart of Your Marriage* is a powerful tool in helping marriages flourish and grow. Dave is able to apply the insightful knowledge he has gained through working with hundreds of couples in counseling. *Getting to the Heart of Your Marriage* will help each couple see their own patterns of behavior, and their unique personality and communication styles that pierce the heart of why they are doing what they do. Dave provides biblical knowledge and simple, practical application that couples may use to restore peace and joy in their marriage. I use the principles in this book in my own counseling practice."

– Peggy Hughes
LPC, *Genesis Christian Counseling*

"In this carefully crafted book, Dave helps us understand the basics of relationship dynamics. You'll likely see yourself in one or more of the portraits painted through its pages. As you read and apply the principles, I believe you'll be encouraged, equipped, and empowered for a healthy, more enjoyable marriage."

– Vincent Newfield
Author and Speaker
New Fields Creative Services

"We have personally experienced Dave's counseling and have been greatly helped through his unique information, method, and biblical foundation. *Getting to the Heart of Your Marriage* reads as if one were actually participating in his counseling sessions. Dave has a distinctive message that speaks to the heart of the marital issues that we all face. I believe that his book should be "required reading" for anyone who is contemplating marriage or even remotely struggling with their marital relationship."

– A former client

DEDICATION

This book is dedicated in memory of my loving mother, Trudy Holden, who sincerely understood what it means to live in a marriage that is founded on commitment and grace, and who modeled to me the fruit of love, joy, peace, patience, kindness and gentleness – attributes that I am certain played into the longevity of her own marriage of 66 years to her one and only husband, my father, Paul Holden.

TABLE OF CONTENTS

INTRODUCTION

FOR OVER TWENTY years, it has been my privilege to serve as a Christian marriage and family counselor. Since embarking on my practice in 1996, I have worked with hundreds of couples from multiple walks of life, helping them overcome the challenges they are facing with their marriage. Along the way, I have witnessed some specific, common patterns that often lead to the struggle and breakdown of marriages. More importantly, I have identified proven remedies to overcome these root issues.

Those who know me and have benefited from my counsel will tell you that I am a "whiteboard junkie." That is, I find it very beneficial to draw things out and write things down for people to view and process in a simple yet memorable way. So as we journey together, we will explore a number of helpful illustrations and diagrams I have developed that provide insights to why couples struggle and how to overcome these difficulties. You will also have opportunity to take the principles we've discussed and apply them in your life through the Q and A section "Making It Yours."

My desire in writing *Getting to the Heart of Your Marriage* is to create a *personalized counseling experience* just for you. As you read, I want you to feel as though I am right there with you, listening and offering relevant answers for the challenges you are facing. I sincerely pray that you will discover just how much God loves you, and that as you invite Him to be the center of your life, He will richly bless your marriage in ways you never imagined!

Dave

PART I

THE "WHY" BEHIND IT ALL

UNDERSTANDING ROOT ISSUES
THAT GOVERN RELATIONSHIPS

"Forgiveness is the only way to break the cycle of blame–and pain–in a relationship...It does not settle all questions of blame and justice and fairness...But it does allow relationships to start over."

—PHILIP YANCEY[1]

CHAPTER 1

FOUR COMMON MARRIAGE SCENARIOS

*For you have been called to live in freedom, my brothers
and sisters. But don't use your freedom to satisfy your
sinful nature. Instead, use your freedom to serve one
another in love. For the whole law can be summed up
in this one command: "Love your neighbor as yourself." But if you are always biting and devouring one
another, watch out! Beware of destroying one another.*

—Galatians 5:13-15 NLT

Jen and Bill
"The Absentee Spouse"

Jen was struggling in her marriage with Bill. She felt totally
alone and isolated in their relationship. As a successful attorney,
Bill spent many hours at his office working on cases. When he
wasn't at work, he would relieve his stress by playing a round of
golf, shooting hoops in his men's basketball league, or hanging
out with his buddies while watching sports at a local restaurant.
Occasionally, he and Jen would go out to dinner or watch a movie together at home. But these times were few and far between.

Periodically, Jen would bring up her concerns to Bill about
the distance she felt in their marriage. When she did, he simply

ignored her comments or made empty promises that they would do something together that weekend. Inevitably, however, something always seemed to 'come up' at the last minute, and Bill would be off and running in a different direction.

As time passed, Jen became more and more discouraged. The possibility of positive change seemed bleak. Feeling hopeless, she went to speak with a counselor regarding her situation.

"I feel totally alone in my own house," she sorrowfully expressed. "It's as if Bill and I are merely roommates living under the same roof. It's like he wants to live a single life and only have me around as a companion when it suits his fancy. This is not what I signed up for in marriage. Something needs to change or I want out."

Kyle and Linda
"The Negative Nag"

Linda was constantly critical of Kyle. Again and again, she voiced her disapproval regarding the inadequacies of his job and the money he brought home. Whenever he did a project around the house, she only commented on what he did wrong and often added, "You really should have hired a professional to do that."

To make matters worse, Linda constantly compared Kyle to other men, expressing how she wished he were more like them. "Oh, if you could just be like 'so-and-so,'" she'd whine. "Life would be so much more enjoyable." Indeed, in Kyle's mind, he couldn't do or say anything to win the approval of his wife.

For the most part, Kyle kept his feelings and frustrations to himself. He did not feel the freedom to be open and honest with Linda. While there were times he mustered up the courage to say something to her, inevitably she would negate his comments and tell him why he was wrong for thinking or feeling the way he did. Deep inside, Kyle knew he was growing apart from Linda. With each condemning episode he became more and more resentful of her. But he just wasn't sure what to do about it.

Overwhelmed, he finally went to speak to his pastor about his situation.

"I feel so down and defeated in my marriage," Kyle said frustratingly. "As a man and a husband, I feel like a complete failure. Linda never seems to have anything nice to say about me. I can't remember the last time she told me she loved me or even had a positive thing to say about me. Being around her depresses me more and more each day. I just don't know how much more of this I can take. Honestly, I think it may be best for us to separate for a while."

JILL AND KEVIN
"THE ANGRY INTIMIDATOR"

Kevin had a problem with anger. When things did not go his way or his wife, Jill, tried to express her concerns about their marriage, he would quickly flare up and become agitated. It wasn't long before Jill became afraid to confront Kevin about anything. When she did muster up the courage to express her frustrations, he quickly got upset, became defensive, and began to intimidate her with angry words. There were even a few occasions when the argument escalated into Kevin violently pushing Jill against a wall.

In desperation, Jill reached out and confided in some trusted friends about her situation. But the opinions and advice she got were mixed. Some would say, "You need to hang in there and be more submissive and supportive of Kevin." While others touted, "You ought to just pack your bags and leave him. You deserve better than that!" There were also a few who suggested that Jill demand they get some counseling to force the issues, and Kevin's anger, out into the open.

Time progressed and Jill did nothing. Consequently, she became more hurt, confused, and afraid. Feeling there was nowhere left to go she turned to her pastor for help.

"I just don't feel safe in my own home anymore," she cried. "Kevin is like a ticking time bomb ready to explode at any minute. I feel like I'm constantly walking on eggshells, trying not to upset him or push the wrong buttons. There's no real freedom for me when he's around. It's as if I'm trapped in a pressure cooker with no way out. Honestly, I am getting more and more afraid of what he might do to me. I think maybe I should just move out."

John and Sally
"The Micro-Manager"

John felt very controlled by his wife, Sally. Whenever he tried to make decisions regarding the house or finances, she dictated what she thought should be done and then gave instructions on how to do it. There always seemed to be an invisible undercurrent of manipulation from her to take her position on issues and give in to what she wanted.

The same thing happened when John was doing something around the house. Without fail, Sally would interrupt him and say, "Please don't do it that way, John. *This way* is how it should be done," and then proceed to demonstrate the "right" way of doing things.

At times she would ask him for his opinion on something but then quickly shoot down his ideas, explaining why his method was just not as good as hers. Greatly frustrated, he would often say, "Why do you even bother to ask me for my opinion when your mind is already made up on what you are going to do?"

Hemmed in and beaten—that's how John felt in his marriage. "It's like I'm a puppet on strings," he periodically commented to his friends. On a few occasions, he angrily lashed out at Sally and called her "controlling," but this only made matters worse. As strange as it may seem, she frequently nagged John about taking more of the leadership role in their marriage and around the house. With each passing day the relationship grew colder and more distant.

Like many others, John went to speak with a counselor about his situation.

"I just don't feel like a man in my own house," he voiced with deep regret. "There is nothing I can do without Sally dictating her desires or telling me how I should do something. She says that she wants me to be the leader in the house, but it certainly doesn't feel that way. How am I supposed to lead when she really wants to be the boss and in control of all the decisions? Her attitude and actions are constantly chipping away at my manhood. Quite frankly, I wonder if we should have ever gotten married in the first place."

So Jen feels totally alone and isolated in her marriage to Bill. Kyle feels constantly criticized and inadequate in his marriage to Linda. Jill feels unsafe and threatened in her marriage to Kevin. And John feels controlled, manipulated, and dictated to in his marriage to Sally.

What do these four marital scenarios have in common? More than you might think. While each of these situations may appear to be different, they are actually very much alike. They all have common roots that are the wellspring of the problems. These roots are the unmet basic longings of each husband and wife— the longings for **value** and **security**. When these go unmet, a marital tug of war results. And that is what we are seeing in each of these scenarios.

REVISITING OUR MARITAL SCENARIOS
JEN AND BILL

Jen feels totally alone and isolated in her marriage to Bill because he spends most of his time at work, playing sports, and hanging out with his friends. Ultimately, she feels as if she is being neglected. What is the bottom line of why she wants a significant change from Bill or out of the marriage? The answer is that *Jen is not feeling valued, appreciated, or loved by Bill.* The less she feels valued and of worth, the more she feels hurt, disappointed, and wanting out.

It's important to note that we do not fully understand what is going on in Bill's life. It may be that he is getting his need for value and worth met at the office. Maybe he is receiving all sorts of praise for his efforts by his coworkers. Or maybe he is getting his sense of worth and/or security from his buddies as they hang out and play sports. It's possible that he doesn't have a good sense of belonging and acceptance from Jen, but he is receiving it from his friends. Thus, he naturally gravitates to spend his time where he gets the greatest payoff. Or maybe Bill is just ignorant to the way a marital relationship should work. He truly wants the best of both worlds in being married and single at the same time.

KYLE AND LINDA

Linda's husband, Kyle, constantly feels criticized by her. Nothing he does appears to be good enough to satisfy her. He feels more and more depressed and defeated each day. Why did Kyle express to his pastor his desire for a separation? Again, the answer goes back to his need for value, worth, and acceptance. Linda's actions constantly chip away at Kyle's worth and value. He rarely, if ever, feels respected, acknowledged, or appreciated by her. In fact, he has finally reached his limit of her continuous negativity and put downs.

On the other hand, Linda may be struggling with her sense of safety, security, and stability. Her lack of personal security and/or need for order could very well be at the root of her constant comments and criticism. She may have also grown up in an authoritative and legalistic household—one in which performing well was required in order to receive love and acceptance. This could be at the root of her "nothing is ever good enough" mentality. Her criticism and negativity towards her husband may very well be coming from her own insecurities and/or need for control over her situations. Sadly, neither Kyle nor Linda is probably aware of these dynamics at work, causing the problems and the breakdown of their marriage.

Let us then pursue what makes for peace and for mutual upbuilding.

ROMANS 14:19 RSV

JILL AND KEVIN

Kevin is the husband who has anger issues, flaring up often and intimidating his wife, Jill, with his angry words and mood swings. On a few occasions he has even reached the point of being physically abusive to her.

Why does Jill feel a strong urge to move out of the house and get away from Kevin? The answer is that she *doesn't feel a sense of safety, security, and stability with him.* She cannot continue to live with a man whose moods and behaviors are unpredictable and bring a continuous sense of physical and emotional instability.

At the same time, Kevin may also have issues with his own sense of value and worth. His anger may stem from his personal feelings of failure and inadequacy as a husband and/or a man. He may also have his own issues with safety, security, and stability. His anger may very well be a form of controlling Jill and their marriage. At the root of abusive and controlling men is often the seed of anger.

It's also possible that Kevin grew up in an unstable and abusive home where he never experienced a sense of safety, security, and stability. We almost always reproduce in our marriage what we personally saw modeled before us during childhood. This may be at the root of his emotional instability and outbursts.

JOHN AND SALLY

John is the husband who feels controlled and manipulated by his wife Sally. Whenever he tries to make a decision or do something around the house, she comments on how it *should* be done. Consequently, John feels compelled to do everything Sally's way.

Ironically, she says that she wants John to lead more, but he feels his hands are tied. From his perspective, he is either *not leading* or *not leading* *"right."* Clearly, he is between a rock and a hard place.

What is fueling the fire of this dynamic in their marriage? The answer is most likely *Sally's need for safety, security, and stability.* Her drive to control her situations and receive assurance pressures her internally (and possible subconsciously) to control her husband and their marriage.

The aftermath of Sally's need for control is John's feelings of inadequacy and a lack of manhood. He senses very little value, respect, or acceptance from her. Because he is feeling so defeated in his marriage, he wonders if he and Sally are even right for each other. Maybe they are just too different and should have never gotten married in the first place. In fact, he is beginning to believe that she needs to go and find someone else who can adequately meet her needs.

Unfortunately, this is a common statement I hear from couples who are struggling with their differences in marriage. Ever since the fall of man, there has existed a basic human struggle for (1) *value, worth,* and *acceptance* as well as (2) *safety, security* and *stability.* The more I counsel couples, the more I run into this relational tug of war over these basic longings. When these are not being protected, guarded, and experienced in marriage, it usually results in significant problems.

Again and again, the couples I work with acknowledge that this is the case. In fact, I would venture to say that if we were to trace the root causes of every divorce, separation, or strained marriage in the history of mankind, it would boil down to one or both partners feeling a lack of value and/or a lack of security within their relationship.

*The more I counsel couples, the more I run into this relational tug of war over the basic longings for **value** and **security**.*

HERE'S HOW RELATIONSHIP DYNAMICS OFTEN WORK

Of all the couples I have worked with over the years, generally speaking, one spouse tends to struggle more with their self-image and sense of value. What they are ultimately looking for is the approval and acceptance of their spouse. They tend to be on the more sensitive (passive) side of the spectrum and often take things personally that are not intended to be personal. They desperately want to avoid criticism, rejection, and feelings of inadequacy. As a result, they will typically keep their inner world to themselves and not share their desires, hurts, or disappointments with their spouse.

Over time this builds emotional distance and possibly resentment toward their spouse who they view more and more as dominant, controlling, and bossy. Keeping their true feelings to themselves may also result in frequent and unpredictable blow-ups. Over time frustration builds as they feel hurt, and they cannot keep their feelings bottled up any longer. They blow-up, get the tension out (through inappropriate words, emotions, or behaviors), and then go back to stuffing their true thoughts and emotions. This would certainly fit the profile of *Kyle* and *John* in our scenarios above.

The other spouse will tend to have a higher sense of need for structure and stability, and often be on the more dominant (assertive) end of the spectrum. What they desire is a life that is in order and situations that are the way they are "supposed to be." To achieve this, they will often abruptly dictate what they think should be done concerning a situation and come across as inflexible regarding their position on issues. They are typically born leaders, and it can be difficult to convince them that any way other than their way is the right way to go. As you might expect, their method of communication often comes across as demanding, harsh, and critical. While it is not necessarily their intent to criticize, they are simply emphatic or "matter of fact" about their opinions. This profile fits *Linda, Kevin,* and *Sally* in our scenarios above.

You can probably imagine the end results of these dynamics. The *more sensitive spouse* will continually feel bowled over and controlled by the more assertive one. They will perceive that they are constantly being told what they do wrong and feel as if they can never do anything right. Consequently, they will also often feel as if they are in a parent/child relationship with their spouse. Thus, in relating to their spouse, they will repeatedly experience their sense of value and worth being chipped away. However, because they want to avoid conflict and being hurt further, they will keep everything to themselves. This cycle will continue and eventually result in an emotional breakdown and detachment on their end of the relationship.

The *more assertive* (less sensitive) one will feel confused and misunderstood as their comments are often taken the wrong way and their spouse gets defensive or relationally retreats. However, they may also be largely unaware of how they are coming across to their spouse. They are oblivious of their abrupt and matter-of-fact communication pattern, their dominance in negotiating issues, and their drive to maintain life according to their point of view. The assertive spouse will also feel confused as to why their mate is progressively disengaging from them relationally and emotionally. They may also have a difficult time handling the "passive-aggressive" behavior of their spouse as their spouse stuffs his or her thoughts and feelings only to blow up or vent their pent up frustrations and anger.

A major key to overcoming these types of relational pitfalls is to understand the way your spouse is wired and how you are wired. With this knowledge, you can learn how you need to work together to protect and preserve your differences and simultaneously, your peace. By being aware of and *preserving* each other's value and security, you can more effectively deal with the issues at hand.

A major key to overcoming relational pitfalls is to understand the way your spouse is wired and how you are wired.

"WHAT DO *I* NEED TO LEARN?"

If you are the MORE ASSERTIVE/LESS SENSITIVE PERSON, you will need to learn to communicate in such a way that does not make your spouse feel devalued, controlled, or minimized (see Chapter 9 for more details). You need to realize that you can often come across as unloving or callous in your sharing of the truth. Since you are more naturally a "take-charge" leader of passion and certainty, you should also be careful of the possibility of fostering a parent/child relational dynamic.

The assertive partner must also learn how to better negotiate issues, come to a compromise, and yield on the "minor" issues of life (see more on this in Chapter 10). If you are more assertive one, you need to realize that your spouse may largely operate the way they do because they struggle with their own sense of value and worth. With this in mind, don't undermine them or tear them down. Instead, look for ways to encourage your partner's value and help them build a proper sense of self-worth. With these guidelines as your aim, you *both* will greatly blessed!

If you are the MORE SENSITIVE/PASSIVE PERSON, you need to understand and inquire about the true motives of your assertive partner. Typically, their motive is not to control, dominate, or treat you like an incompetent child. They are simply operating on how they view situations and life. You also must be careful not to misinterpret your spouse's comments and make negative, false assumptions. Be sure you have all the facts and that you are not getting upset over something they do not mean or intend.

Here's something else to keep in mind. If your more assertive spouse truly does struggle with their own sense of security and stability, you need to be aware of this and help your partner build and maintain their security, not work against it. The assertive spouse's ultimate goal is self-protection and building a sense of personal security. Finally, as the more sensitive partner, learn how to work through any hesitancy to speak up. To have and maintain a healthy relationship, get your thoughts, feelings, and opinions out on the table, and quit living in fear of your spouse. We will take a closer look at these relational dynamics as we explore personality differences in relationships in Chapters 4 and 5.

BE REAL AND HONEST WITH YOURSELF

All this being said, I believe we all have a responsibility to be real and honest with ourselves. That is, ask yourself the hard questions of **why** you tend to do what you do, and face your own potential issues of a lack of value and/or security. I believe that the more confident we are in our own sense of value and security and draw upon God's love and sovereignty for our ultimate value and security, the better we can navigate relationships. The less confident we are, the more we will tend to feed off each other to protect our own deficiencies. In the coming chapters, I will discuss where the true and absolute source of our value and security should lie.

CHAPTER SUMMARY 1

Most marital problems have common roots. These roots are the unmet basic longings of each husband and wife—the longings for **value** and **security**. When these go unmet, a marital tug of war results. A major key to overcoming these pitfalls is to understand the way your spouse is wired and how you are wired, and then learn how to work together to protect and preserve your differences and your peace.

(1) Quotes on Relationships, *Daily Christian Quote* (http://www.dailychristianquote.com/?s=relationships, retrieved 1/25/16).

Making It Yours ———————————————————

1. Of the four marriage scenarios presented, is there one that you seem to identify with most? If so, which one? Why do you feel this is the case? What helpful insights have you learned to apply in your own marriage?

———————————————————————

———————————————————————

———————————————————————

———————————————————————

2. Without question, the home environment in which you grew up has a strong influence on how you interact with others when you become an adult—especially your spouse. Take a few minutes to sit quietly and recall the atmosphere of your home life as a child and teen. Then take time to describe...
The Overall Environment

———————————————————————

———————————————————————

The Interaction Between Your Parents/Guardians

———————————————————————

———————————————————————

How Conflicts Were Handled between Your Parents/ Guardians

———————————————————————

———————————————————————

As you are reflecting, pray. Invite God into your present situations and ask Him to reveal and heal any pain from your past. Is there anything specific He is showing you about your past? Are there any actions you sense you should take?

_____

_____

_____

_____

3. It is very important to understand how your spouse is wired and what makes them feel truly valued and safe. From your perspective, complete the following statements:
My spouse feels value, worth, and acceptance when...

_____

_____

My spouse feels safe, secure, and stable when...

_____

_____

Once you have recorded your answers, ask your spouse to complete the statements about themselves. How well did you answer for them? What did they share that was different from your responses?

_____

_____

_____

18

"All of us are wounded, imperfect, broken sinners who do not have the ability to love another wounded, imperfect, broken sinner the way we need to in the relational furnace called marriage. The shortest route to a godly marriage and family is to first invest the ongoing effort and time each day in becoming a more passionate, committed, and skilled disciple of Christ."

—DENNIS RAINEY[1]

CHAPTER 2

TWO BASIC NEEDS EVERY HUMAN HAS

*...And I pray that you, being rooted and established
in love, may have power, together with all the saints,
to grasp how wide and long and high and deep is the
love of Christ, and to know this love that surpasses
knowledge—that you may be filled to the measure of all
the fullness of God.*

—EPHESIANS 3:17-19

EVERY PERSON—REGARDLESS OF their nationality, background, or
personality—has two basic longings. The first is a longing to be
loved, valued, and accepted, and the second is to feel safe, secure, and stable.

When I think of these two driving desires, I am reminded
of the story in Scripture of the Israelites and their journey out
of Egyptian bondage. For over 400 years, the descendants of
Abraham had been enslaved. In the midst of their severely harsh
treatment, God heard their cry and delivered them in grand
style, bringing ten miraculous plagues of judgment against the
Egyptians and opening the Red Sea for their safe passage toward
the Promised Land.

The people of Israel were spellbound by God's awesome
demonstration of power, love and protection, rejoicing in song

over what He had done. Scripture records, "The Lord saved Israel that day from the hand of the Egyptians, and Israel saw the Egyptians dead on the seashore. When Israel saw the great power which the Lord had used against the Egyptians, the people feared the Lord, and they believed in the Lord and in His servant Moses" (Exodus 14:30-31 NASB).

Ironically, only forty-five days later, Israel's celebration turned into murmuring and complaining. When their supply of food and water was depleted, they immediately began to grumble against Moses.

"Why did you bring us and our families out here to starve?" they whined. "Were there not enough graves in Egypt for us to stay there and die? At least we had food to eat and water to drink!"

The truth is, the people were not murmuring against Moses. Ultimately, their griping was against God. What was at the root of their complaints? In essence they were asking two basic questions: First, "Does God care about us? Does He truly *love* us? Do we really have *value* to Him?" And second, "Is God really able to take care of us and keep us *safe* out here in the wilderness?" Israel, like many of us, was questioning God's power, provision, knowledge and capabilities.

How are Our Needs to be Met?

Why write this snippet of Israel's history? Because I believe it is a clear example that demonstrates the two basic needs all human beings grapple with: a need for **value**, **worth**, and **acceptance** along with the desire to feel **safe**, **secure**, and **stable**. As a counselor, I encounter many people wrestling with these needs in their personal lives and relationships as well.

In my practice, and even in my personal experience, I have witnessed that when we have our personal value and security firmly established in our relationship with God, we are able to navigate life and the potential challenges it brings. However, when we are weak in our personal sense of value and/or security, we tend to compensate for this lack in several ways.

As I have worked with hundreds of married couples, I have frequently witnessed the relational tug of war that takes place as they attempt to preserve and meet these basic needs for value and security. Surprisingly, most couples are not even aware that this dynamic is at work in their relationship.

But whether they are aware of it or not, it can make or break their marriage, building up or tearing down their *House of Intimacy*, which we will discuss in the chapters ahead. Therefore, it is vital to understand what these needs are, how you and your spouse are uniquely wired, and then work together to foster and protect these needs within your marriage.

When we have our personal value and security firmly established in our relationship with God, we are able to navigate life and the potential challenges it brings.

THE NUMBER ONE NEED:

VALUE, WORTH, ACCEPTANCE

As human beings living in a fallen world, we each have a longing for *value, worth,* and *acceptance*. Words that convey the meaning of value, worth and acceptance include: significance, usefulness, meaning, respect, acknowledgement, appreciation, and recognition. You and I need to believe that we have and experience this vital sense of meaning and dignity. Whether we consciously realize it or not, we yearn to feel accepted, loved, and affirmed by those around us, particularly our spouse. Everyone needs a place where they experience a true sense of community and belonging, and marriage is an incubator in which this awareness may grow.

If we are in a relationship in which we continually do not feel valued, acknowledged, or appreciated, we will soon begin to disconnect from that person emotionally. Kyle from Chapter 1 is a prime example of this. He felt that his wife, Linda, was constantly critical of him and very rarely had a positive or encouraging thing to say. He didn't feel valued, appreciated, or respected by Linda. Over time, Kyle began to feel discouraged in his marriage and relationally disconnected from Linda. Ultimately, he was protecting himself from something most people greatly fear—rejection.

---

*As human beings living in a fallen world, we each
have a longing for value, worth, and acceptance.*

AVOIDING REJECTION

In some ways we all struggle with our personal sense of value. If we are honest with ourselves, we will admit that there are areas of our lives in which we feel insecure. However, when people lack a significant sense of value and worth, it drives them to protect their ego—their personal sense of self-image. Ultimately, they are trying to protect themselves from feelings of failure or rejection.

To be rejected is to take a personal hit on our feelings of value, worth, and acceptance. If we are living in this mode, our motivation for relationships (and life in general) will be to avoid rejection and potential failure of any kind. This is often done unconsciously by avoiding activities in which we might fail as well as avoiding people and relationships in which we may experience conflict or not be accepted. Clearly, we don't want to be hurt or hurt others. The result is living in a world motivated by a fear of others—possibly even our spouse. This lack of authentic living and the continual avoidance of dealing with issues eventually lead to emotional disconnection.

While no one likes to be rejected, some have a heightened sensitivity to rejection. These are people who significantly lack their own sense of value and worth and often question God's love and acceptance. For them, life progressively moves on a predictable path that looks something like this:

Root Problem	An Inner Struggle	Ultimate Outward Goal
a lack of value → →→ and self-worth	to preserve one's ego →→→ (dignity and self-image)	to protect oneself from failure and rejection

Those of us who live in this self-protective mode use certain relational tools to safeguard our value, worth, and acceptance. Our tools of choice are: Pleasing Others, Proving Ourselves, and Protecting Ourselves.

PLEASING OTHERS

By attempting to please and accommodate others, we are actually trying to assure that we will not be rejected. *Who is going to reject me if I please them and make them the center of my attention?* We might say to ourselves. Sadly, if we are people pleasers, we cannot say "no" to anyone. We think, *To say no might mean that someone will be disappointed in me or upset with me.* So, rather than risk disappointment or rejection, we live a life of simply making everyone around us happy and avoiding anything that might lead to rejection.

People pleasers are also often prone to give up their own wants continually for the sake of accommodating others and making them happy. While it is important and at times healthy to compromise, a repeated pattern of sacrificing one's desires will turn into resentment and bitterness, leaving oneself feeling the opposite of what is desired—minimized and dismissed.

If you are married and living in this manner, you will tend to avoid relational conflict with your spouse at all costs. This can be very detrimental to maintaining a healthy emotional connection in your relationship as we will see more clearly in the chapters ahead.

...We do not aim to please men, but to please God who knows us through and through.

1 THESSALONIANS 2:4 J.B. PHILLIPS

PROVING OURSELVES

Another way we tend to avoid rejection is by continually trying to prove our worth and value to others through our actions and accomplishments. "Look what I did!" is our battle cry, regularly drawing attention to ourselves in an attempt to convince others, and ourselves, that we are not failures. The problem with this method of gaining acceptance is that we are constantly on a *performance treadmill,* and we are only as good as our last accomplishment.

If you are living your life trying to prove your worth and value to others, you are probably experiencing an emotional roller coaster of successes and failures. If you succeed, you feel worthy and you are "up." If you fail, you feel unworthy and you are "down." More than likely, you are striving to be a "perfectionist." The goal of perfectionism is to minimize mistakes and failures, avoiding criticism and rejection. Perfectionism is an emotionally tiring and unrealistic world to live in.

Striving for *excellence* is a healthier, more attainable motivation. Excellence is doing the best you can with what you have—be it time, material, and/or talents. If you find yourself struggling for perfection, give yourself a break. Do your best, and then trust in God's remarkable character with the rest! That is, learn to tap into His amazing love, patience, and grace each day. His Word invites us to "Come to me, all you who are weary and burdened, and I will give you rest. Take my yoke upon you and learn from me, for I am gentle and humble in heart, and you will find rest for your souls. For my yoke is easy and my burden is light." (Matthew 11:28-30 NIV). It is often that the perfectionist expects more from self in the trivial matters in life than God Himself requires.

PROTECTING OURSELVES

The third tool of choice we tend to use in hopes of gaining and maintaining our worth and value is self-protection. We do this mainly through avoidance. We will go out of our way to avoid anything or anyone that might lead to rejection. By avoiding conflict we hope to keep others, including our spouse, from being upset.

We think, *If I hide my true desires, hurts, and frustrations from others, they will not be disappointed in me or upset with me.* Accordingly, we play it safe by keeping our true thoughts and feelings to ourselves. If we are not careful, living with this mindset will lead to bitterness, resentment, and even more emotional disconnection.

We also seek to protect our sense of worth and value by avoiding anything that might lead to failure. By only engaging in activities, tasks, and relationships where we know we will succeed, we minimize our chances of failure. What this achieves, however, is living in a world of self-protection—a world that lacks authentic relationships and is littered with missed opportunities.

Are you beginning to see how living with this approach in marriage will totally discourage intimacy? If you habitually avoid conflict, shying away from conversations in which you must be vulnerable and live in a world of fear and self-protection, you will not grow close to your spouse or to those around you. Instead, you will become overly sensitive to what is happening relationally, particularly with your spouse. And because you are fearful of giving and receiving truth, you will often misinterpret others' intentions, making negative and false assumptions, habitually becoming upset over what I call "non-reality."

What is the better way to live? God's Word instructs us to, "...lovingly follow the truth at all times—*speaking truly, dealing truly, living truly*—and so become more and more in every way like Christ who is the Head of his body, the Church. Under his direction, the whole body is fitted together perfectly, and each part in its own special way helps the other parts, so that the whole body is healthy and growing and full of love" (Ephesians 4:15 TLB).

*...Lovingly follow the truth at all times—speaking
truly, dealing truly, living truly—and so become more
and more in every way like Christ who is the Head of
his body, the Church.*

EPHESIANS 4:15 TLB

THE NUMBER TWO NEED:

SAFETY, SECURITY, AND STABILITY

A second need we have as human beings is a need for *safety, security,* and *stability*. Words that express the meaning of safety, security, and stability include: protection, safekeeping, refuge, sanctuary, steadiness, firmness, and strength. You and I need to feel a sense of safety and security as we interact with others and navigate through situations in daily life. We need to experience a sense of stability and believe that we have some form of power or control over our lives and our destinies.

If we are in a relationship where we constantly feel a sense of insecurity and instability, we will eventually want to flee that relationship to higher ground. That was Jill's situation in Chapter 1. She did not feel safe with her husband Kevin's emotional and physical outbursts. Her feelings of insecurity and instability led her to want to separate from their marriage.

Similarly, if someone is in a marriage where they continually feel controlled and dominated by their partner, they will not feel like an equal partner in the relationship. Eventually they will pull away emotionally. This was John's position in Chapter 1. He felt manipulated, controlled, and suppressed by his wife Sally. The "Johns" I work with in counseling will often tell me that they feel like an empty shell, and that they have lost their sense of self. They also state that they feel as if they live in a parent-child relationship with their spouse. Again, this discourages and shuts down the desire to draw closer as a couple.

The truth is, all of us wrestle in some way with our sense of security and stability. No one is a perfect fortress of strength and confidence. Consequently, we all tend to be motivated to some degree to protect our emotional or physical well-being from loss or harm. This need may also drive us to establish and maintain order, structure, and control in our world. This is especially true for those who have experienced a chaotic or abusive background. We create a rigid, clear-cut, self-protective environment whereby we have as much predictability and security as possible. For others, this rigidity is simply the outflow of growing up in a strict, dominant, and authoritarian home where there was little room for diverse opinions or error. Still for others, it may simply be the product of their nature (personality) and how they view, process, and handle situations and life.

Whatever the case, the end result is knowingly or unknowingly seeking to control everyone and everything around us. The control may be subtle and come through suggestions, persuasion, and manipulation. In more severe cases, the control is more blatant and manifests as insistence, dominance, and intimidation.

The person on the receiving end is left with little freedom and input into matters of the relationship. Indeed, a one-sided and controlling relationship will definitely undermine intimacy in a marriage.

While everyone has some sense of need to control certain aspects of their lives, others have a heightened sensitivity to direct things. For those who significantly lack a personal sense of safety and security, life progressively moves on a predictable path that looks something like this:

ROOT PROBLEM	AN INNER STRUGGLE	ULTIMATE OUTWARD GOAL
a lack of safety, → →→	to preserve oneself →→→	to protect oneself from
security, and stability	emotionally and physically	any loss or harm

The way many people seek to protect their safety, security, and stability is by seeking to create a predictable world in which they ultimately control everyone and everything around them. The more we seek to control our lives, situations, and environment, the more we feel safe and secure. Unfortunately, when we live this way, our spouse often ends up feeling the brunt of our drive for order, structure, and control. Instead of being united as one, we end up divided and growing further apart.

Those of us who live in this self-protective mode use certain relational tools to preserve our safety, security, and stability. In this case, our relational tools of choice are: Ensuring Predictability, Managing Predictability, and Controlling Predictability.

A second need we have as human beings is a longing for safety, security, and stability.

ENSURING PREDICTABILITY

To ensure our safety, security, and stability, we often strive to make certain that everything around us is predictable and operating according to our plan. The *more* that everything is precisely the way we want it, the *more in control* of our life we feel. The *less* that things are the way we want it, the *less in control* of our life we feel. What's the result of the latter? We experience a lack of personal peace and tranquility.

People who are driven to *ensure predictability* are what I call the "box" people. If life remains neatly inside their box, they feel safe and secure. If life breaks outside their box, they feel insecure and will do whatever they can to get their life back inside the box. Again, predictability brings them security.

MANAGING PREDICTABILITY

The methods we use to ensure that our world is the way we want it is what I call *managing predictability*. By managing everything and everyone around us, we attempt to orchestrate our world in a way that makes our lives as predictable as possible.

Those who live this way seem to have a comment for everything and suggest or insist that something be done the way *they* think it should be done. Sally from Chapter 1 is a perfect representation of this way of thinking. She was constantly stating her opinion of how things should be by telling John what to do. The net result is Sally relentlessly orchestrating a predictable world, but John emotionally checking out of the marriage.

CONTROLLING PREDICTABILITY

The driving force behind managing and ensuring predictability is the need to *control* situations and others. Through the use of control we attempt to get others to conform to our agenda. The more others conform to our agenda, the more we have assurance that everything is the way it should be. The less others conform to our agenda, the less we feel that things are the way they should be and the less safe, secure, and stable we feel.

This approach to relationships—the controlling approach—will not encourage intimacy and oneness in marriage. One of the key aspects of intimacy, which we will discuss more in Chapter 6, is developing a true partnership. The essence of a partnership is in setting goals *together,* making decisions *together,* and charting life *together.* If one spouse is operating in control, attempting to manage and control everything in the relationship, the other will not feel like a partner in marriage. The controlled one will eventually build resentment and emotional distance from the controlling one.

Another potential pitfall of being driven by control is setting up a parent/child form of relationship. The partner who feels controlled will often tell me that they feel more like a child in the marriage than a spouse. If you find yourself being the dominant, controlling person, you need to stop and honestly ask yourself, *What is the root cause for my tendency to control things?*

OPPOSITES ATTRACT

You have probably heard it said of marriages that opposites attract, and it is very true. I also find this to be the case when it comes to fulfilling our two basic needs. Very often I see someone who has a greater sense of need for value and approval (a more passive and laid back person) married to someone who has a greater sense of need for stability and structure (a more dominant and assertive person). This factor can be a significant challenge if each partner does not understand how they are wired and learn to get a handle on the dynamics of their relationship.

The *passive, sensitive partner* who lacks a sense of value and worth will continually feel devalued, manipulated, and controlled by their spouse's dominance and agenda. More often than not, they end up feeling that they can't do anything right or measure up to their spouse's constant desires, demands, or standards. However, rather than getting their true thoughts and feelings out on the table they will keep everything locked inside. Over time they will distance themselves relationally from their spouse. They will also have a tendency to misinterpret their spouse's motives or comments and take them as a personal attack, although that was not the intention. If left unchecked, this will eventually produce an emotional disconnection from the relationship.

The *dominant, assertive partner* who lacks a sense of safety and security will feel even more insecure and confused as their spouse disengages from them. The more assertive spouse will often communicate that they feel their spouse will not be open with them and actively discuss issues. Because of their mate's patterns of passivity and inability to handle situations, they will also begin to lose respect for them, especially if the passive one is a man. To make matters worse, the dominant partner will also become confused and feel misunderstood as their spouse unexpectedly and abruptly blows up over an issue. However, the more assertive spouse will also often be unaware of how they are communicating to their partner, coming across as harsh, abrupt and demanding.

If not addressed, this dynamic will continue to chip away at the couple's *House of Intimacy* and deteriorate the spiritual and emotional connection they experience within their marriage. I have personally witnessed this dynamic over and over again in the couples I have worked with.

THE BOTTOM LINE

I said it at the opening of this chapter, and I will say it again. It is my firm belief that the ultimate solution to this human struggle for value and security is to know—*really know*—who God is and learn to firmly trust in Him for our value, our security, and our very existence. It is revealed in Scripture that "Those who know your name will trust in you, for you, Lord, have never forsaken those who seek you" (Psalm 9:10).

Since the dawn of creation, God has intended for us to have these needs ultimately met in our relationship with him. He is the Almighty, All-Sufficient One! As our heavenly Father, He desires and is certainly capable of being the true Source of our value and our security. And He is definitely One to keep His Word!

CHAPTER SUMMARY 2

As human beings, we all have two basic needs: the first is a sense of value, worth, and acceptance, and the second is a sense of safety, security, and stability. In marriage, there is often a relational tug of war that takes place over these two basic needs. God, our heavenly Father, desires and is certainly capable of being the true Source of both these needs. When we have our personal value and security firmly established in our relationship with Him, we are able to navigate life and the challenges it brings. If we try to satisfy our needs and insufficiencies in our own ability, it will lead to distancing and emotional disconnection in our relationships—especially in our marriage.

(1) Dennis and Barbara Rainey, *Starting Your Marriage Right* (Nashville, TN: Thomas Nelson, Inc., 2000, p. 104).

Making It Yours ────────────────────────────

1. The two basic needs that all humans have are *value, worth,*
    and *acceptance* as well as a need for *safety, security,* and *stabil-*
    ity. Of these two needs, which seems more important to you
    personally? To the best of your ability, explain why this is the
    case.

    _____

    _____

    _____

    _____

    Of these two needs, which do you think is more important to
    your *spouse*? To the best of your ability, explain why you feel
    this is the case.

    _____

    _____

    _____

2. From your perspective and to the best of your ability, com-
    plete the statements that follow:
    I feel VALUED and LOVED most by my spouse when they...

    _____

    _____

    I feel SAFE and SECURE most by my spouse when they...

    _____

    _____

    My SPOUSE feels VALUED and LOVED most by me when
    I...

    _____

    _____

My SPOUSE feels SAFE and SECURE most with me when I...

_____

_____

_____

Once you have answered questions 1 and 2 on your own, sit with your spouse and ask him or her to answer the same questions from their perspective. How are your answers similar? Where are they different?

3. While we are all made to serve and meet each other's needs, God is the One who ultimately desires and is capable to provide for us. The question is, do you believe this to be true? Do you personally know that God loves *you* and deeply desires to meet *your* needs and be in relationship with you? Carefully read through these passages and write down what He reveals to you.

    Matthew 11:28-30; Revelation 3:20; Romans 8:31-32, 35-39

_____

_____

_____

Psalm 34:4-10; 84:11; Philippians 4:19; 2 Corinthians 9:8

_____

_____

_____

Psalm 91 and 121; Isaiah 41:10-13

_____

_____

_____

"The good news is that we weren't meant to succeed by depending only on each other. Marriage is a triangle—with husband and wife at the bottom corners and the Lord at the top. ...If we invite the Lord into our marriage and trust in His strength, we can experience strength and peace in our marriage regardless of the circumstances."

—Dr. James Dobson[1]

CHAPTER 3

THE TRUE SOURCE OF VALUE AND SECURITY

Your love, O Lord, reaches to the heavens, your faithfulness to the skies. …Oh Lord, you preserve both man and beast. How priceless is your unfailing love! Both high and low among men find refuge in the shadow of your wings.

—PSALM 36:5-7

AT THIS POINT, I would like to take some time to focus and reflect on where our personal sense of value and worth, as well as our security and stability, should ultimately come from. It is clear that problems develop when we relationally interact with our spouse through our own insecurities. When we look to him or her to fulfill certain needs that they may not be capable of fulfilling, there is bound to be trouble.

GOD IS...

OUR ULTIMATE SOURCE OF VALUE, WORTH, AND ACCEPTANCE
To whom or what should we look to for our validation and significance? The answer is ultimately God. He created us inside

and out. He was there when we were being formed in our mother's womb. He knows our thoughts before we think them and our words before we speak them. He knows everything about us and is certainly concerned about our destiny and well-being (see Psalm 139).

There is no one and nothing like our God! He never changes (see Hebrews 13:8). God is the only true constant we have in our life. He is the only One who will "*never leave us or forsake us,*" as we read in Deuteronomy 31:6 and again in Hebrews 13:5.

Just how valuable are you and I in God's eyes?

Through David He declares,

> *O Lord, our Lord, how majestic is your name in all*
> *the earth! When I consider your heavens, the work of*
> *your fingers, the moon and the stars, which you have*
> *set in place, what is man that you are mindful of him,*
> *the son of man that you care for him?*
> *You made him a little lower than the heavenly beings*
> *and crowned him with glory and honor. You made him*
> *ruler over the works of your hands; you put everything*
> *under his feet; all flocks and herds, and the beasts of*
> *the field, the birds of the air, and the fish of the sea, all*
> *that swim the paths of the seas. O Lord, our Lord, how*
> *majestic is your name in all the earth.*

—PSALM 8:1, 3-9

Interestingly, some interpret this passage to mean that man should consider himself to have very little significance in the sight of God. They wrongly render the phrases "what is man that you are mindful of him, the son of man that you care for him?" as saying, "When I consider the awesomeness of Your power and creativity and the magnitude and brilliance of Your creation, what is man that You care for him? He is but a fleeting breath of insignificance that is not even worthy of Your notice or attention." However, nothing could be further from the truth.

If we are true to the context of this passage in its entirety, the interpretation should be rendered that man has *great* significance in the eyes of God. And the place of importance He has conferred on us in His creation is *top priority*.

With this accurate perspective, the true meaning of this passage should be interpreted as, "Wow! When I consider the awesome works of Your hands and the magnitude of Your creation, I am astounded at the significance You have given me as Your treasured creation! You have made me a little lower than the angels. You have crowned me with glory and honor and have made me ruler over Your creation and placed everything under my care. Thank You, God, for the intense love You have for me as Your treasured creation!"

God is the only true constant we have in our life.
He is the ultimate Source of our value, worth, and
acceptance.

YOU ARE CHOSEN BY HIM!
Another passage in which God reveals our great value to Him is Deuteronomy 7:6-8. In it He proclaims,

For you are a people holy to the Lord your God. The Lord your God has chosen you out of all the people on the face of the earth to be his people, his treasured possession. The Lord did not set his affection on you and choose you because you were more numerous than other peoples, for you were the fewest of all peoples. But it was because the Lord loved you and kept the oath he swore to your forefathers that he brought you out with a mighty hand and redeemed you from the land of slavery, from the power of Pharaoh, king of Egypt.

In this passage we again see the significance we have to God and the deep love He has for us as His *treasured possession.* If you are a Christian, you are a member of God's family! He personally chose *you* because He loves you, and you have significant value to Him!

In Jeremiah 1:5 (AMP) He declares,

Before I formed you in the womb I knew and approved of you [as My chosen instrument], and before you were born I separated and set you apart....

In Ephesians 1:4 (NLT) He reveals,

Even before he made the world, God loved us and chose us in Christ to be holy and without fault in his eyes. God decided in advance to adopt us into his own family by bringing us to himself through Jesus Christ. This is what he wanted to do, and it gave him great pleasure.

And in John 15:16, Jesus Himself states,

You did not choose me, but I chose you and appointed you to go and bear fruit—fruit that will last....

God did not choose you and me because we are a great people. He did not choose us because we are endowed with incredible gifts and abilities. He chose us simply because He loves us. You and I have incredible value and worth to Him, just like the people of Israel.

As a Christian, you are a member of God's family! He personally chose you because He loves you, and you have significant value to Him!

DO NOT FEAR WHAT PEOPLE THINK

Because of your circumstances you may be struggling to experience God's love and acceptance for you. However, the truth is that God does love you and always has your best interest in mind even if you cannot see it or understand it. In reality, He is the only One who can give you true value, worth, and acceptance. He is the only One who can consistently love you in a way that you need it and can receive it. To look to receive our value, worth, and acceptance anywhere else—even from our spouse— is to set ourselves up for grave disappointment.

The truth is, when we place more stock in what people think and say about us than what God does, we are living under "the fear of man." This flawed way of living grants others power and control over our lives they were never meant to have. Indirectly, they become the arbitrator of our worth and value. In actuality: "Fear of man will prove to be a snare, but whoever trusts in the Lord is kept safe." (Proverbs 29:25 NIV).

I have found that people who struggle with their sense of value and worth also struggle with feeling valued, loved, and accepted by God. This was me to a tee when I was in my teens and early twenties. I worried greatly about what other people thought of me. I desperately wanted everyone to like me and accept me as a person. To achieve this I spent much of my time trying to please everyone and make them happy. I could not say "no" to anyone. To do so might mean they would be disappointed in me and not like me. Consequently, I often took on too many commitments and attempted to be too many things to too many people.

Avoiding conflict of any kind was another major symptom of my fear of man. I never brought up my needs, wants, hurts, or frustrations to anyone. I would rather suffer internally than suffer someone's rejection. I simply hated when others were angry or upset with me. Add to all this, I was a big-time perfectionist. I spent many fruitless and wasted hours on trying to make everything I did perfect. Years later I learned that my perfectionism was actually my way of avoiding criticism and being considered an incompetent failure. The bottom line is that I was looking to others for my sense of value and worth. At my own admission, I let others hold my value and worth in the palm of their hands.

I am telling this part of my personal story to encourage you. If you are struggling with the fear of man like I was, there is hope! What I have just shared took place years ago, and I no longer look to others for my value and worth. I ultimately get my value and worth met through my relationship with God and my acceptance in Him. I am convinced that God loves me and that I have value to Him.

As a result, many transformations have taken place in my life since then. First, I am no longer gripped by fear of what others think about me. While I definitely welcome constructive criticism (something I desperately avoided in the past), I do not care if people like and accept me. I do not need the acceptance and approval of others for my sense of value and self-worth.

Second, I no longer avoid conflict. I am comfortable being open and honest in dealing with people and situations. I am willing to get things out on the table and deal with them. The craziest thing of all is that I now do mediation work and get in the middle of other people's conflicts for a living! Indeed, God does seem to have a sense of providential humor.

Third, I am no longer a perfectionist. While I used to have a preoccupation with everything being perfectly in order, I am no longer that way. I have come to realize and accept the difference between doing a job adequately and overkill. I have exchanged perfectionism for striving for adequate *excellence*. I have discovered that there is great peace in doing your best and then resting in God's love, acceptance, and grace with the rest.

Fear of man is a dangerous trap, but to trust in God means safety.

PROVERBS 29:25 TLB

YOU HAVE PURPOSE AND MEANING IN HIM

As I mentioned previously, two words that describe and define worth and value are *purpose* and *meaning*. As human beings created in the image of God, we all have a need for purpose and meaning. We all want to feel a sense of usefulness in the world in which we live. If we consistently lack a clear sense of purpose and meaning, we can definitely become depressed. This is one of the indications I look for when I work with people who are dealing with depression. Do they feel they have purpose and meaning in life?

"What should our purpose and meaning be founded on?" you ask. "From where should we draw our significance?" Good questions. As Christians, God gives us great purpose and meaning through the greatest commandment He gave us. Jesus Himself quoted it in Matthew 22:37-39:

> "...Love the Lord your God with all your heart and with all your soul and with all your mind." This is the first and greatest commandment. And the second is like it: "Love your neighbor as yourself."

When Jesus recited these instructions from the books of Deuteronomy and Leviticus, He reiterated the true source of our purpose, meaning, and significance in life. Like all aspects of our worth and value, purpose and meaning ultimately flow from **loving God** and **loving others**. There is nothing more internally fulfilling.

Whenever we hear about someone who has faced severe adversity in life and overcome it, we also typically hear how they have received renewed strength and wisdom through the ordeal. They have found something outside of themselves that gives them a great sense of purpose and meaning—a new drive for life. They are no longer obsessed with themselves or their hardship. Instead, they are passionate about reaching out and loving others with their newfound mission.

On the contrary, people who are depressed are often very self-absorbed. Thinking about and reaching outside of themselves to help others is very difficult. They are too busy being preoccupied with self. Personally, when I am obsessively focused on loving and taking care of myself, I begin to lose my sense of joy and peace. Yet, as I spend my time loving and serving God and others, I have a renewed sense of joy, peace, and meaning in my life. I believe this is a significant key to internal contentment that few people find. I also believe this is why the "love of self" is so often at the foundation of the breakdown in a marriage.

Is it any wonder God repeats the essence of His greatest commandment through the apostle Paul in the book of Galatians? To make sure we don't miss our primary purpose for living, He says,

> *You, my brothers, were called to be free. But do not use*
> *your freedom to indulge the sinful nature; rather, serve*
> *one another in love. The entire law is summed up in*
> *a single command: "Love your neighbor as yourself."*
> *If you keep on biting and devouring each other, watch*
> *out or you will be destroyed by each other.*

—GALATIANS 5:13-15

These are great words of wisdom that I often use in marriage counseling. I tell couples that we are free—free to make the choices we want to make. We can use our freedom to love and care for one another, or we can use our freedom to bite and devour each other. The end result of the latter is that we destroy each other and our relationship. Sadly, this is what happens in too many marriages. Biting and devouring typically comes from our own selfish desires that wage war within us.

Again, God's Word clearly reveals this:

> *What causes fights and quarrels among you? Don't they come from your desires that battle within you? You want something but don't get it. You kill and covet, but you cannot have what you want. You quarrel and fight. You do not have, because you do not ask God.*

—JAMES 4:1-2

The bottom line of most fights and quarrels in marriage is that we want something and we are not getting what we want. When we become angry with our spouse a good question to ask is, "What is it that I want that I am not getting?" In the end, how can we overcome this ungodly tendency to fight and quarrel with our spouse and others to try to get what we desire? We must go to God and ask Him for what we need and for Him to cultivate within us the ability to live a life of love and humility, considering our spouse and others as "better than ourselves." The only way to cultivate true love is to gradually and inwardly let go of self. There is no magical formula, pill, or step-by-step procedure to weed out selfishness and self-centeredness. It is a slow process of dying to self. Put simply, the more we hold on to self and selfish desires, the less we will grow in love. **Jesus said, "If anyone**

wants to be first, he must be the very last, and the servant of all" (Mark 9:35). This is the only true way to weed out needless fights and quarrels.

Purpose in life ultimately flows from loving God and loving others. There is nothing more internally fulfilling.

GOD IS...

OUR ULTIMATE SOURCE OF SAFETY, SECURITY, AND STABILITY
To whom or what should we ultimately look to for our protection and safekeeping? Again, the answer is to look to God. He is sovereign—that is, He has supreme rule and no one is greater or higher than Him.[2] He is also All-Powerful, All-Knowing, and All-Present. In other words, He is everywhere at all times and has all the power, knowledge, and wisdom needed to oversee our lives adequately and fulfill His purpose for our lives.

How safe and secure are you under God's care? Read what King David proclaims:

I love you, O Lord, my strength. The Lord is my rock, my fortress and my deliverer; my God is my rock, in whom I take refuge. He is my shield and the horn of my salvation, my stronghold. I call to the Lord, who is worthy of praise, and I am saved from my enemies.

—PSALM 18:1-3

Find rest, O my soul, in God alone; my hope comes
from him. He alone is my rock and my salvation; he is
my fortress, I will not be shaken. My salvation and my
honor depend on God; he is my mighty rock, my refuge.
Trust in him at all times, O people; pour out your
hearts to him, for God is our refuge.

—PSALM 62:5-8

Four times in these six verses, we hear David describe God as his "Rock." Three times he refers to Him as a "Refuge," and three times David says God is our source of "Salvation." Now this is coming from a person who was being hunted down like an animal by a madman and his army for over a dozen years. Multiple times David was in the grips of death, yet miraculously delivered. If anyone could stand and give account of God's reliability and power to keep us safe and secure, it is David.

In Psalm 46 the sons of Korah write,

God is our refuge and strength, an ever-present help
in trouble. Therefore we will not fear, though the earth
give way and the mountains fall into the heart of the
sea, though its waters roar and foam and the moun-
tains quake with their surging.
The Lord Almighty is with us; the God of Jacob is our
fortress.
Be still, and know that I am God; I will be exalted
among the nations, I will be exalted in the earth.
The Lord Almighty is with us; the God of Jacob is our
fortress."

—PSALM 46:1-3, 7, 10-11

Like David, the sons of Korah were looking to God as their ultimate source of safety, security, and stability. He was their fortress and their refuge. He was their strength, protection, and stronghold, and He is the same for us. To look to anyone or anything other than God for our safety, security, and stability is to put our life in the hands of something or someone that cannot ultimately deliver.

God is All-Powerful, All-Knowing, and All-Present.
He is our ultimate source of safety and security.

CAN YOU IDENTIFY WITH JIMMY?

Many people struggle to feel safe and secure, and so did "Jimmy." He was about fourteen years old and suffering from a social phobia when I started working with him. He would not leave his room or his house. Every time he was faced with having to leave home, he would go into a panic. He was afraid that if he left, something terrible might happen to him. As long as he stayed at home in his room, he felt a sense of control and security that nothing bad would befall him. The resulting problem was that he was isolated, lonely, and unable to go to school, which was a necessity.

The root of Jimmy's problem was that he was struggling with his sense of safety, security, and stability. The only way he felt safe and secure was to retreat from society and stay at home. Rather than risk any harm, he decided to take matters into his own hands and rely on his own wisdom and abilities for security.

Of the many things that I worked on with him, I attempted to help him see that his life was ultimately in the palm of God's hands, and that not a hair would fall from his head apart from

God's will (see Matthew 10:29-31). People who struggle with their sense of safety and security often struggle with relying on God's power, providence, and sovereignty. As a result, they feel compelled to control their own lives to ensure their physical and emotional safety as much as possible.

So where am I going with all this? As I mentioned in Chapter 2, I have witnessed that those who ultimately find their value and security in their relationship with God are endowed by Him with their own sense of value and security. Overall they maintain life and relationships well. However, when one or both partners in marriage have significant value and/or security issues, they will find life and relationships more challenging.

I am also convinced that to the extent a marital couple is polarized in regard to their longings for value and security, the more challenging their relationship will be. This is certainly what I have experienced in my counseling practice. While one spouse is somewhat secure and stable, the other may struggle greatly with their sense of value. The spouse who struggles to feel valued will tend to be more dependent, indecisive, silent, and yield their decisions away. They will also consistently misinterpret and misunderstand the more secure spouse, seeing them as more demanding, controlling, and critical than they really are.

At the same time, one spouse may have a strong sense of self-worth and value, but the other may have significant security issues. The insecure spouse will be largely motivated to protect their physical and emotional well-being by seeking to dominate and control their circumstances, and hence, the more stable spouse. They will also be more adamant that their spouse successfully live life inside their security "box."

Of course one of the worst scenarios I have witnessed is when a spouse with significant value issues is married to a spouse with significant security issues. This is a recipe for marital disaster unless they come to some sense of mutual understanding, acquire some helpful relational tools, and develop the ability to work together.

When one or both partners in marriage have significant value and/or security issues, they will find life and relationships more challenging.

No Man Is an Island

Remember the words I wrote in Chapter 2 that convey experiencing a sense of safety, security, and stability? They were: protection, safekeeping, refuge, sanctuary, steadiness, firmness, and strength. As we have literally seen these words in our Scripture verses above, and would witness in numerous other Scripture verses, God is the only true Source that we may depend on for our very life.

Even so, though we should ultimately look to God for our value and worth, as well as our security and stability, we still need each other. We are not islands. We are all humans with relational, emotional, and physical needs. God created us as relational beings meant to live out our lives authentically in community.

No matter how spiritually strong or mature we are, we all need to feel that we matter to others and that we are secure in our environment. In few places is this reality more important than in a marital relationship between a man and a woman. That is why I keep driving home the point that as couples, we need to look to protect each other's sense of value and security at all costs. The reality is, by nurturing and protecting your spouse's value and security you are actually preserving your marriage and protecting your own sense of value and security.

CHAPTER SUMMARY 3
Our personal sense of worth and value, as well as our security and stability, ultimately come from God. He is the only true constant stabilizing factor we have in our lives, and He loves us beyond what we can fathom. Each of us has purpose and meaning in Him, and it ultimately flows from loving Him and loving others. As we draw our value and security from our relationship with God, He will become a solid foundation in our lives and empower us to consider and protect our spouse's longings for value and safety. In this there is great marital reward!

(1) Dr. James and Shirley Dobson, *Night Light* (Sisters, OR: Multnomah Publishers, Inc., 2000, p. 90). (2) Adapted from *The New Unger's Bible Dictionary*, Merrill F. Unger (Chicago, IL: Moody Press, 1988, p. 1214).

Making It Yours ————————————————————————

1. You are chosen and deeply loved by God! He has personally selected you to be a part of His family through Jesus Christ. Carefully read the following passages. How do God's words in these verses encourage you and make you feel valued by Him?

   I Am Chosen by God: Jeremiah 1:5, Isaiah 49:1; John 15:16

   _____

   _____

   _____

   I Am Loved by God: John 3:16-17; Romans 5:8; Ephesians 2:4-5; 1 John 3:1; 4:9-10

   _____

   _____

   _____

2. The "fear of man" is a deadly, dangerous trap. The question is, are you caught in its grips? Read through this brief evaluation and answer each question as honestly as you can.

   Using the numbers 1 through 5, place a number in the space next to each question that best answers it.

   (Number **1** = Never; **2** = Seldom; **3** = Sometimes; **4** = Often; **5** = Always)

   _____What others think, feel, and say about me (their opinion) is extremely important.

   _____I find it difficult to say "no" to others when asked to do something.

   _____When it comes to helping others, I'm over-committed, often while the important things in my life go undone.

_____ I am uncomfortable being open and honest about my feelings. I'd rather keep them to myself.

_____ I avoid conflict with others at all costs.

Now add up the numbers. If you scored between 5 and 10, you are probably not influenced much by the fear of man. If you scored between 10 and 15, the fear of man has a mild to moderate influence. If you scored between 20 and 25, the fear of man is likely dominating your life. Pause and pray, asking God to reveal anything you need to see about yourself and Him.

3. Knowing that our sense of value and security ultimately come from God, it is important for both you and your spouse to develop a healthy relationship with Him. In what ways can you encourage your wife/husband to invest in and cultivate their relationship with God? What could you do together to draw closer to Him?

I believe I can encourage my spouse to cultivate a healthy relationship with God by...

_____

_____

Together, my spouse and I can draw closer to God by...

_____

_____

"The couples who make it in marriage are not carbon copies of each other. They are people who have learned to take their differences through the process of *acceptance, understanding,* and eventually *complementation*. Differing from another person is very natural and normal and can add an edge of excitement to a relationship."

—**H. NORMAN WRIGHT**[1]

CHAPTER 4

UNDERSTANDING THE DYNAMICS OF PERSONALITY

You made all the delicate, inner parts of my body and knit me together in my mother's womb. Thank you for making me so wonderfully complex! Your workmanship is marvelous—how well I know it.

—PSALM 139:13-14 NLT

"TOM," SAID JENNIFER. "I need you to stop and pick up some groceries on your way home from work."

Eager to serve his wife and make her happy, Tom willingly obliges Jennifer and stops at the local market on his way home. After conquering the crowds and gathering the goods he was asked to secure, he walks into the house with groceries in hand.

"Hey honey, I'm home," Tom announces. "I got the groceries you asked for." With a sense of success, Tom places the bags of groceries on the counter.

Then it happens.

"Aw, Tom!" Jennifer abruptly exclaims while unpacking the bags. "You got the wrong rolls!"

"Oh why do I even bother?" Tom mutters under his breath as he turns and stomps up the stairs. "I can't do anything right.

Every time she asks me to do something, I do it wrong. I can never make her happy. I can't even buy the right bread!"

I wonder what's eating him? Jennifer says to herself as she hears Tom abruptly close the bedroom door.

Sound familiar? This is a typical scenario that plays out in households across the land. It is actually a picture of personality differences and how they can affect relationships.

As I have worked with hundreds of people over the years, I have developed my own personality continuum that describes how individuals are wired and what makes them tick. I have found that personality differences are often the "tail that wags the dog" in marriages as well as virtually every relationship that exists. I have also discovered that these personalities largely flow from the two basic needs for value and security that we addressed in Chapter 2.

Personality differences are often the "tail that wags the dog" in marriages as well as virtually every relationship that exists.

I break my personality continuum down into three categories: Personality Types, Basic Character Traits of Personalities, and the Driving Forces behind Personality Traits.

CATEGORY 1

FOUR PRIMARY PERSONALITY TYPES

These include Passive, Laid-Back, Assertive, and Aggressive. The continuum looks like this:

Passive-----------------**Laid-Back**-----------------**Assertive**------------------**Aggressive**
(Avoiders/Accommodators)   (Matter of fact/Attackers)

"PAT"

THE PASSIVE

Passive people are the avoiders in life. They do not like conflict. They would rather sweep disagreements under the rug and hope they go away. If you ask these people what is wrong, they will typically say, "Nothing is wrong," or, "I don't want to talk about it."

Passives also tend to be overly sensitive. They are more easily offended and hurt by the words and actions of others. They also lean towards being more dependent and indecisive. When it comes to making decisions, they need the opinions of others before making a final choice. Ultimately, passive people are driven by a mission to make everyone happy and avoid rejection. They are the people pleasers of life and find it hard to say "no" to anyone.

"LARRY"

THE LAID-BACK

A second personality type is what I call *Laid-Back*. These people are often the happy-go-lucky accommodators in life. They are just a few steps away from being passive. They do not necessarily avoid conflict, but they also do not take life very seriously. They let things roll off them like water off a duck's back. Laid-Backers are *not* primarily motivated to make everyone happy. However a situation turns out is okay to them; they really don't care.

For example, if you ask them where they want to go out to eat, they will usually reply, "It doesn't matter to me. You decide.

I really don't care where we go." Laid-Backers often make light of crucial situations because they simply don't see the severity of the issue. This is usually not because they are trying to avoid issues. It is more likely the result of simply not seeing the importance of it.

"ANGELA"

THE ASSERTIVE

Assertive people are your "matter of fact" ones. While they are not over the top aggressive, they are typically self-confident and not afraid to freely express their opinion or give feedback. They are processors and thinkers who weigh the facts and core information of a given situation and then make logical decisions.

Assertives are upfront and honest with just about everyone. For instance, they won't hesitate to say something like, "That shirt really doesn't look good on you." Comments like these are not necessarily motivated by criticism, control, or wanting to have their own way. They are just being honest based on how they see things. As you might expect, they often unknowingly offend people with their straightforwardness.

"AARON"

THE AGGRESSIVE

The fourth personality type is *Aggressive*. These people are the attackers in life. They will often emphatically and dogmatically express their opinion as if it is the unshakeable truth. It is absolutely critical that others see matters their way. They often intimidate people with their abrupt outward emotions and actions. In the end, their goal is often to control people and situations around them. They are the micromanagers of people and life.

Having a disagreement with an aggressive person often feels like arguing a case with a prosecuting attorney. "You did not say that!" they will exclaim. "*This* is what you said. Clearly, *you* are in the wrong here!" Soon your head is spinning and you feel pinned against a wall. Being right and winning the argument appears to be the Aggressive one's driving motivation. They seem far less concerned about resolving things peacefully. They are probably best described as the proverbial "bull in the china shop."

I have found that there are four basic personality types: Passive, Laid-Back, Assertive, and Aggressive.

Now that we have examined a basic definition of the four personality types, let's examine the character traits uniquely linked with each.

CATEGORY 2

BASIC CHARACTER TRAITS OF PERSONALITIES

These are the natural qualities occurring in people on each end of the continuum. While Laid-Back people tend to exhibit a varying degree of the Passive personality traits, Assertive individuals tend to demonstrate a varying degree of the Aggressive personality traits.

Passive--------------------Laid-Back-------------------Assertive------------------Aggressive

- sensitive
- relationally-driven (you/me)
- more people-driven
- subjective
- dependent
- more emotional (feeler)
- flexible
- indecisive
- strives to make everyone happy

- things are black/white
- more task, issue-driven (it)
- more principle-driven
- literal; puts things in a box
- independent
- more logical (thinker)
- inflexible; loves routine
- decisive
- appears stable

BASIC CHARACTER TRAITS OF

THE PASSIVE/LAID-BACK PERSON

Sensitive: Passive/Laid-Back (P/LB) people tend to be more sensitive and get their feelings hurt more easily. Their sensitivity causes them to want to avoid being hurt or hurting others. Thus, they tend to suppress their true thoughts and feelings and avoid being honest with people. They often take things personally that are not meant to be personal.

Remember Jennifer's comment to Tom in the opening scenario—that he bought the wrong rolls? Her remark was not actually meant to be personal. She was not trying to attack Tom and his capabilities. She was simply focused on the rolls (the "it"). In his sensitivity, Tom took the comment and made it a personal issue (you/me).

Relationally-Driven: P/LB people tend to be more relationally-driven. Ultimately, everyone being happy is most important.

It doesn't really matter who is right and who is wrong, as long as everyone feels good about the situation in the end. People and their feelings are more important than issues. Tom did not care about buying the right bread. He simply wanted his wife, Jennifer, to be happy with him.

Subjective: According to the P/LB person, there is more than one way to do things. Everything does not need to be exact. If they are ten minutes late to something, it doesn't really matter. They are close enough to being on time.

There is also not always a clear right and wrong in situations. For the P/LB, there are at least two roads to get to a desired destination, and it really doesn't matter which road you take. They both end up at the same place.

Dependent: Overall, P/LB people tend to be more dependent. They often find it hard to make decisions without getting the opinions of others. They also tend to be more dependent in their relationships. That is, they want others to be happy or "okay" with them. They will often relinquish their decisions to others for the sake of peace.

More Emotional: The P/LB person tends to be more emotionally-driven than logically-driven. They are "feelers" more than thinkers. When people are upset with them or they are upset with others, they tend to retreat or become very emotional.

Flexible: This is a typical characteristic of P/LB people. They do not need to have things their way and are very accommodating to the thoughts, desires, and opinions of others. A downside to being flexible is that they will often give up their own wants and opinions too quickly in order to make others happy.

Flexibility may also be a device a P/LB person employs to avoid conflict or avoid someone being upset with them. Eventually, this can turn into resentment toward others—a feeling of "never really having a say in matters."

Indecisive: Along with the P/LB's dependence comes a tendency towards indecisiveness. They often struggle and take a long time thinking things through before making a decision. They tend to shy away from taking risks. They want as many i's and t's dotted and crossed before making a commitment and moving forward. This is typically done to avoid making a mistake.

Strives to Make Everyone Happy: The ultimate goal of the P/LB person is to ensure that everyone is happy. As long as everyone is happy, they feel good about themselves and situations.

Passive and Laid-Back people tend to exhibit similar qualities. They are sensitive, dependent, and people-driven individuals who strive to make everyone happy.

BASIC CHARACTER TRAITS OF

THE ASSERTIVE/AGGRESSIVE PERSON

Black and White: The Assertive/Aggressive (A/AG) person tends to view all issues as either black or white. To them there is a clear right and wrong way to act in almost every situation. For example, if you are driving from point A to point B, there is only one good way to go and all others ways are ultimately the wrong way.

When an A/AG person is convinced they are right about something, it is very hard to change their mind. Jennifer, in our opening scenario, had one specific kind of bread roll in her mind that she wanted. All other rolls were the "wrong rolls." If she had taken time to communicate to Tom the specific type of rolls she wanted, he would have likely succeeded in getting the "right" ones.

Task/Issue-Driven: Instead of being relationally (people) driven, the A/AG person is prone to being more focused on tasks and issues. While the Passive/Laid-Back person is more concerned with "you and me" and how we *feel* about a situation, the A/AG person is more concerned about "it" (the issue at hand).

Making sure "things are the way they should be" trumps how everyone *feels* about the task or issue. For example, Jennifer was more concerned about the bread ("it") than Tom's feelings. Tom, on the other hand, was more concerned about everyone's feelings ("you/me") than the bread.

Principle-Driven: The principle of a matter is what propels an A/AG person. How people feel about an issue is of little or no consequence. "As long as things are 'the way they should be,'" I often hear them say, "as long as the principle (or the issue) is right, that's all that matters."

Literal: The A/AG person tends to process issues more literally than subjectively. That is, they say what they mean and mean what they say. They take people at face value and literally bank on what others say to them.

"You told me you would be home at 6:00 p.m.," the Assertive/Aggressive spouse might say. "That is when I was expecting you. It's now 6:10 p.m. Where have you been?" In this case, the A/AG's literal perspective creates an inflexible mindset that will likely lead to problems.

Independent: Unlike the Passive/Laid-Back person who often depends on others to make decisions, the A/AG person has a propensity to be independent and often acts autonomously from others. Many times they will make a decision, act on their decision, and process the decision with others later. When an

Assertive/Aggressive person and their Passive/Laid-Back spouse take a trip to the store, the independent A/AG partner is often walking toward the door or in the store before the P/LB is even out of the car.

Logically-Driven: The A/AG person is more logically-driven than emotionally-driven. In other words, they are thinkers and processers of information rather than followers of their feelings. In order for them to buy into something, it has to make sense to them—it has to be the *logical* way to go. A/AG people spend more time thinking issues through and logically coming to conclusions than getting emotional over them.

Inflexible: Because A/AG people view issues as more black or white and are more logically- driven, they may be perceived as inflexible. They often come across as having a "my way or the highway" mentality. It is as if they are saying, "There are two ways to do things: My way and the wrong way." While this attitude is usually not specifically verbalized, it is the unspoken impression given by the A/AG person.

Decisive: The A/AG person is typically very decisive. They know what they want and don't hesitate to go after it. They are often "knee jerk" responders and risk takers. Typically, they make decisions quickly, and process their decision later. The downside of this is that they may act before they really think the issue through.

Assertive and Aggressive individuals tend to demon-strate the same traits. They are task-driven, decisive, independent people who are more concerned with issues than feelings.

CATEGORY 3

THE DRIVING FORCES BEHIND PERSONALITIES

What drives all these personality types? Why do they think what they think and do what they do? What is in their hearts, motivating them to act and react the way they do?

Passive--------------------Laid-Back--------------------Assertive------------------Aggressive

DRIVEN BY:	DRIVEN BY:
Need for approval	Need for order, structure, control
Fear of failure and rejection	Fear of emotional or physical loss or harm
Value-based issues	Security-based issues
At the end of the day they are looking for:	At the end of the day they are looking for:
Acceptance and Validation	Exactness, Predictability, and Security

WHAT TYPICALLY DRIVES THE PASSIVE PERSONALITY?

What is the driving force in the heart of the passive person? Why do they do what they do? As I have worked with many people on the passive end of the spectrum (and used to be the poster child for it myself), I have found that they are often motivated by: (1) a need for approval, (2) a fear of rejection, and (3) a fear of failure.

THE NEED FOR APPROVAL

The passive personality is typically motivated by a *need for approval* from others. They want everyone to like them and be happy with them. This longing for approval forms the basis for their sensitivity, indecisiveness, flexibility, and dependence. Ultimately, the goal of the passive person is to gain acceptance and avoid the disapproval of others. In marriage, Passives desperately seek the acceptance and avoid the disapproval of their spouse.

THE FEAR OF REJECTION

Another motivation of the passive person is the *fear of rejection*. They want to avoid being rejected or rejecting others at all costs. This is largely why they avoid conflict and withhold their true feelings from others. To avoid conflict means to avoid being hurt or hurting others. To the Passive, receiving constructive criticism, disappointing someone, or having a disagreement are all forms of rejection. In marriage, the passive person often keeps their inner-truth to themselves.

THE FEAR OF FAILURE

The passive personality is also motivated by a *fear of failure*. In their eyes, to fail means that they are not worthy. Therefore, they procrastinate or avoid anything that may lead to failure or a lack of success. They are typically the perfectionists of life, and their perfectionism is often an attempt to avoid rejection by simply being "perfect" at everything. As I mentioned previously, this was certainly the case with me in my teens and early twenties.

These are the general character traits of the Passive/Laid-Back person and the typical driving forces motivating them to do what they do. At the end of the day, what they are looking for is acceptance and validation. This flows from potential issues with their personal sense of value and self-image. Now let's focus our attention to the other end of the personality continuum.

Passive and Laid-Back people tend to be driven by a need for approval as well as a fear of failure and rejection.

WHAT TYPICALLY DRIVES THE AGGRESSIVE PERSONALITY?

What is the motivating force in the heart of an aggressive person? Why do they do what they do? As I have worked with many people on the aggressive end of the spectrum, I have found that they are often driven by: (1) a need for order, structure, and control and (2) a potential fear of emotional or physical loss or harm.

THE NEED FOR ORDER, STRUCTURE, AND CONTROL

No matter how you slice it, the aggressive personality is looking for everything to be exactly the way they think it should be. If something is out of place, they will make a comment or suggest that things be changed to suit their way of seeing things.

I often refer to aggressive people as the "box" people. They want life to fit neatly inside their box. When life is inside their box, they are content and at peace. If life gets outside of their box, they look for ways to get it back in. They do this by suggesting that things be done their way or by pressuring and demanding people to adopt their position.

THE FEAR OF EMOTIONAL OR PHYSICAL LOSS OR HARM

For some aggressive people, they are very afraid of not having order, structure, and control. To these people controlling their situations feels like a matter of life or death. To *not* have control means complete loss of security and safety. Therefore, it becomes imperative for the Aggressive to control people and situations in order to maintain their sense of security and stability. To maintain control means to avoid any potential physical or emotional loss or harm. This brand of aggressive people often grew up in an abusive or highly chaotic and unstructured background.

For others, having order and control is not so much driven by a fear of emotional or physical loss or harm. Instead, it is the outflow of how they view matters and life. This brand of aggressive people often grew up in legalistic or authoritarian households. Their perspective creates an uneasy feeling, a rigid logical thought process, or an inability to comprehend things not being "way they should be." If you ask them why it needs to be a certain way, they will reply, "It's just the way it is supposed to be," or, "It's the logical conclusion of how things should go." It can be very difficult to convince this person that another way is actually a better way to go.

A third category is those who are simply wired to think more logically and factually, and tend to be more bent toward issues and tasks. They do not necessarily have any abuse in their past. They did not grow up in an authoritarian household. They are simply more assertive and keen on structure by nature. However, as I have mentioned before, we all need to ask ourselves the hard questions of why we think the way we think and why we do what we do to get to the honest roots of our nature and personality.

These are the general character traits of the Assertive/ Aggressive person and the typical driving forces motivating them to do what they do. At the end of the day, what they are looking for is exactness, predictability, and security. This flows from potential issues with their security.

Assertive and Aggressive individuals tend to be driven by a need for order and control as well as a fear of emotional or physical loss or harm.

In the next chapter, we will dive even deeper into the dynamics of the personality continuum.

Chapter Summary 4

Personality differences are often the "tail that wags the dog" in marriages and virtually every relationship. There are four basic personality types: Passive, Laid-Back, Assertive, and Aggressive. Each has certain character traits associated with it. While Laid-Back people tend to exhibit a varying degree of the Passive personality traits, Assertive individuals tend to demonstrate the Aggressive traits. And each personality has unique driving forces motivating them to do what they do. These driving forces typically flow from value and/or security issues.

(1) H. Norman Wright, *The Secrets of a Lasting Marriage* (Ventura, CA: Regal Books, A Division of Gospel Light, 1995, p. 118).

Making It Yours ————————————————————————

1. Of the four personality types—Passive, Laid-Back, Assertive, and Aggressive—which one seems to best describe *you*? How about your *spouse*? What character traits do you (and your spouse) exhibit that confirms your analysis?

    I believe the _____ personality type best describes me.

    The character traits I exhibit are...

    _____

    _____

    _____

    I believe the _____ personality type best describes my *spouse*.

    The character traits he/she exhibits are...

    _____

    _____

    _____

2. In light of your personality, what characteristics do you see as *strengths*? What are some possible *weaknesses* you should be mindful of? List some practical steps you can take to guard against these weaknesses surfacing and hurting your spouse or others.

    The STRENGTHS of my personality include...

    _____

    _____

    _____

    The possible WEAKNESSES of my personality are...

    _____

    _____

    _____

Some PRACTICAL STEPS I can take to avoid hurting my spouse and others are...

_____

_____

_____

3. Unity is powerful! God tells us to "*live in harmony* with one another; do not be haughty...readily **adjust yourself to [people, things]** and give yourselves to humble tasks. Never overestimate yourself or be wise in your own conceits" (Romans 12:16 AMP). Bearing in mind this verse and the differences in personality between you and your spouse, how might you "adjust yourself" to live in more harmony with him or her? (Think about your communication and your thoughts toward your spouse.)

_____

_____

_____

_____

With each question, pray and ask the Lord for His wisdom and insight. He is able to see things in you and your spouse that you cannot see. He will give you the strength to make the needed adjustments and experience a greater level of joy and peace in your relationship than you could ever imagine.

"We're all a blend of four basic personality types, but most of us have one or two dominant styles. Our individual blends make us unique, like fingerprints. And one of the best ways to improve our relationships is to bring balance to any of our traits that we've neglectfully or subconsciously pushed to an extreme."

—GARY SMALLEY[1]

CHAPTER 5

ASSESSING AND ADDRESSING OUR PERSONALITY CHALLENGES

*...Work out the salvation that God has given you with
a proper sense of awe and responsibility. [Not in your
own strength] for it is God Who is all the while effectu-
ally at work in you [energizing and creating in you
the power and desire], both to will and to work for His
good pleasure and satisfaction and delight."*

—**PHILIPPIANS 2:12-13**
(J.B. PHILLIPS/AMPLIFIED)

As YOU READ through the last chapter, you probably saw yourself
somewhere on the continuum. Please realize that in using the
spectrum I presented, I am describing the more extreme case
scenarios of the passive and aggressive personalities. I am depict-
ing the passive person as an overly sensitive, overly emotional,
dependent, indecisive, and avoidant personality. Similarly, I am
describing the aggressive person as a very black and white, inflexible, dominant, literal-thinking, controlling, and attacking
personality.

Therefore, I encourage you not to automatically assume that you or your spouse is one of the extremes. More than likely you are both somewhere in between the two.

FINDING YOURSELF IN THE MIX

Many people tell me, "Dave, I have some traits from both the passive side of the spectrum and the aggressive side." This is quite normal. So, again, do not pigeonhole yourself one way or the other. While most people operate largely out of one side of the spectrum (either predominantly passive or aggressive), many exhibit a mix of traits from both sides for various reasons. In the end, it all boils down to how your value and/or security have been uniquely affected or compromised through living out life in a fallen world. Generally speaking, value issues breed passivity and avoidance, while security issues breed dominance and control.

If you tend to be on the more passive end of the spectrum, it does not necessarily mean that you are motivated by a fear of rejection and a need for approval. Likewise, if you are on the more aggressive end of the spectrum, it does not necessarily mean that you are motivated by a fear of emotional or physical loss or harm. Each of us usually has motivating factors that are unique to us. That being said, regardless of where you and I find ourselves, we all need to be honest and look to see what is really motivating our attitudes and behavior.

So how do we end up more on one end of the spectrum or the other? If you are more passive or laid-back, why is that the case? What is motivating your behavior? If you are more assertive or aggressive, what is the underlying cause? Why do you have a need or bent towards order, structure, and control?

While most people operate largely out of one side of the personality continuum, many exhibit a mix of traits from both sides.

What influences one person to be passive and another to be more aggressive? I believe the answer largely goes back to our two primary needs for value and security that we addressed in Chapters 2 and 3. While it's true that hereditary factors may play a role, I believe that people and their personalities are primarily shaped by external influences more than simply being born with them.

Negative Influences That Lead to Passivity

LACK OR ABSENCE OF AFFIRMATION AND ENCOURAGEMENT

In my observations of working with people, I have found that those who grew up in an environment in which they rarely received positive affirmation and encouragement often end up on the more passive end of the spectrum. For some, there was not only an absence of praise, but also the presence of put downs. Again and again, they were bombarded with negativity and criticism.

"All my parents ever told me was that I was worthless and I couldn't do anything right," many have confided in me. "You'll never amount to anything," is the message countless people heard throughout their growing years. Sadly, some people have even told me that their parents said that they were sorry they had even had them.

Add to this, more criticism, ridicule, and a general lack of acceptance from peers at school and elsewhere and it is no wonder some people are struggling with their sense of value and worth. Negative influences like these set the stage for individuals to be motivated by a deep fear of rejection and failure as well as an avoidance of anything that may rock their fragile world of value, worth, and acceptance.

LITTLE OR NO PERSONAL DECISION-MAKING

Another potential influence that molds people into passivity is growing up in an environment in which everything was done for them, or they were instructed and encouraged in what to do in every situation. While the instruction and encouragement may have been subtle and covert, not blatant or demanding, it still left a harmful impact. Conditions like these ultimately create a more dependent personality in which an individual does not learn to think or fend for themselves. Instead, they learn to depend on others to help them deal with issues and make decisions.

If we don't learn how to think through situations for ourselves and make independent decisions, we will develop a fear that we won't make right decisions. Consequently, we will constantly seek the advice, opinions, and approval of others to minimize the chance of doing something wrong or failing in our choices. Couple this fear of failure with a desire to please everyone and make them happy and you have the classic passive, dependent, and overly-sensitive personality.

INCORRECT CRITERIA OF WORTH

A third potential influence I have seen (and personally experienced) that drives people to the more passive end of the spectrum is what I call an individual's "criteria of worth." These are spoken and unspoken standards that shape one's personal belief system (self-image) as to what makes us have worth and value.

When I was in high school, the following four things were my criteria for personal worth and value: (1) being a three-letter sports person (basketball, baseball, and football); (2) being a jock; (3) being tough; and (4) having big muscles. These were environmental messages I got from my peers, coaches, and others. Unfortunately, because I had none of the above, I had a low sense of value and worth. It would be many years before I would discover that my sense of worth and value was not the problem. It was the faulty criteria on which I was basing my worth and value.

Today, I believe I hold and maintain an accurate, biblical criterion for my value and worth. As a result, I do not struggle with my sense of self-worth. Do you know the criteria on which you are basing your worth and value? If you don't, I would highly encourage you to take the time to determine it. You may be surprised to discover the heart beliefs and attitudes driving your sense of personal worth and value.

Negative influences that lead to passivity include a lack or absence of affirmation and praise, as well as incorrect criteria for your personal worth and value.

NEGATIVE ENVIRONMENTS THAT LEAD TO AGGRESSIVENESS

While some conditions help produce a more passive personality, other conditions lead to the development of an aggressive one. In all my years of counseling, I have typically found that more aggressive individuals grew up in one of three different environments:

CATEGORY 1

GROWING UP IN AN UNSTABLE, CHAOTIC, ABUSIVE ENVIRONMENT

The first category consists of those who grew up in an unstable, chaotic, or abusive environment. These individuals place a high premium on safety, security, and stability. Not having order, structure, and control makes them feel extremely uncomfortable. They live to maintain a predictable and structured environment to ensure their safety and stability. To do this, they are more assertive at streamlining their views, opinions, and wants. For many who find themselves in this category, not having a situation be exactly the way they want it can literally become a matter of life or death in their minds.

Can you see how someone who grew up in an extremely emotionally, physically, or sexually abusive environment would operate this way? If you grew up in an unstable setting like this, you can probably better understand why control, order, and predictability mean safety to you. And how not having control places you at risk for potential physical or emotional loss or harm as you experienced in the past.

CATEGORY 2

GROWING UP IN A DOMINANT, AUTHORITARIAN, LEGALISTIC ENVIRONMENT

A second category is made up of individuals who grew up in a highly dominant, authoritarian, or legalistic environment. Their upbringing was very rigid; they were constantly and blatantly told what to think and do. Directly and indirectly, they repeatedly heard the message that there is *one* way to do something and only one way. All other ways are wrong.

If this atmosphere describes the home in which you grew up, you probably developed a very "black and white" perspective on life. It is also very likely that at least one or both of your parents or guardians dominated you, leaving you little room for creativity or freedom of choice. Furthermore, you may also have gotten the message that if you didn't do something the "right way," you were not in God's will or you jeopardized your faith and right standing with Him. This is essentially legalism. Legalism is ultimately a mentality of exchanging "works" for acceptance, value, and salvation.

I am grateful to say that nothing could be further from the truth! Your worth and value are *not* based on what you do or have done. It is based on what Jesus did. God loves and values you and me so much that He sent His Son to pay the penalty for our sin and restore our relationship with Him.[2] "For it is by grace you have been saved, through faith—and this not from yourselves, it is the gift of God—*not by works*, so that no one can boast" (Ephesians 2:8-9).

81

God loves and values you! Your worth is not based on what you do or have done. It is based on what Jesus did.

CATEGORY 3

GROWING UP IN AN INTELLECTUAL, LOGICAL, FACTUAL ENVIRONMENT

The third category is comprised of individuals who grew up in a more intellectual, logical, and factual environment. They take each situation, look over the information and facts, and come up with a logical conclusion of what should be done. These individuals are not necessarily driven by a need to maintain a safe environment or by a legalistic mentality. For them, it is simply woven into their fiber to make logical, concrete choices based on principle and what seems to be right.

The challenge for people who fall into this category is that it is difficult for them to negotiate and move away from their position on an issue if it doesn't make sense to them. The end result is that others around them feel dominated and controlled.

Are you beginning to see some of the factors that have helped form your personality? Is it becoming clearer as to why you have a tendency to act and react in certain ways? Indeed, understanding how we are wired is a major key to knowing where and how we need to adapt and adjust ourselves in our relationships—especially in marriage.

CLEARING UP SOME COMMON MISCONCEPTIONS

Before going further, let me clear up some common misconceptions, starting with the passive-aggressive personality. While it appears this person has a "split" personality, I believe they are actually more on the passive side of the spectrum. Rather than getting things out on the table, the passive-aggressive person initially stuffs their true thoughts and feelings. Over time, they heat up like a pot of water coming to a boil. They let things fester and build up until they can't keep it inside anymore. Then usually without warning, they boil over, acting out with inappropriate words and/or behavior. Once the pressure has been relieved, they go back to stuffing their true thoughts and feelings again until they reach another boiling point.

How about the passive person? On the surface, it appears he is the *good* guy, and the aggressive person is the *bad* guy. If we simply look at their personalities on paper, the passive person is sensitive, relational, and flexible with the honorable goal of making others happy. On the other hand, the aggressive person is black and white, literal, inflexible, and more concerned with issues than the feelings of others. However, to get an accurate assessment of each personality, we have to look below the surface. There we will find that both the passive and aggressive personalities have their challenges.

More often than not, I find that the aggressive person is misunderstood. They are frequently thought of by the passive person as the one who "makes an issue out of everything" and "won't let go of anything." They are also often seen as constantly stirring up trouble. The truth is, however, in most cases they are simply lobbying for what they believe is right or trying to create dialogue over impending issues. The passive person, on the other hand, would generally prefer to sweep issues under the rug and not deal with them. They blindly hope difficulties will simply go away or work themselves out on their own.

So where is the balance? How do we navigate these relational waters? The answer lies in each of us knowing the inherent challenges in our personalities and working with God and each other to overcome them. As I mentioned previously, I used to be an incredibly passive person. Since God has graciously enabled me to work on and overcome my underlying value issues that drove my passivity, I have become much more assertive in relationships and decisions.

The way we navigate our relationships is by knowing the inherent challenges in our personalities and working with God and each other to overcome them.

HELPFUL INSIGHTS FOR THE AGGRESSIVE PERSON

#1 DISCERN EACH ISSUE'S TRUE LEVEL OF IMPORTANCE

If you identify with the aggressive personality, here are some insights that have helped many of the couples I have worked with.

One apparent challenge the aggressive person seems to have is an inability to discern the true level of importance of issues accurately. From the brand of toothpaste used to significant financial decisions, they appear to treat every matter with the same weight and zeal. They come across as if there is a right way and a wrong way for everything, and the way *they* see things is the way it "should be handled." This leaves others, including the aggressive person's spouse, feeling as if they never have any good ideas or that they can never do anything right. It also makes the aggressive one seem inflexible, demanding, and controlling.

So, how do we discern the difference between the issues we face? Issues of **high-level** importance are those dealing with such things as safety, health, morality, ethics, and significant financial decisions. Issues of **medium-level** importance are ultimately a matter of preference. These include things like the brand of car you buy, the type of house you purchase, or the neighborhood in which you live. **Low-level** importance issues are largely insignificant in the grand scheme of life. These might include things like the color shirt that you wear, the pair of shoes you buy, or the brand of toothpaste you use. A key to remember as the more aggressive person: learn to let go of the little things and focus more on the major issues of life.

#2 GUARD AGAINST BEING ABRUPT OR ATTACKING

As an aggressive individual, another tendency to guard against is being too abrupt or verbally attacking. While the goal of processing through issues and coming up with logical solutions is admirable, the aggressive person will often quickly release their opinion on an issue and, if they are not careful, bowl others over in the process. They are prone to speak first (vent their opinion) and ask questions and process information later. As a result, others may be offended even though there was no offense intended.

Over time people feel may as if the aggressive person is not "safe" to approach with wants or issues.

Interestingly, it is often the aggressive person's abruptness and way of communicating that is the problem, not their information or motivation. I often have the spouse on the receiving end say, "It is not *what* they say that bothers me, but *how* they say it!" How important is our body language, our attitude, our words, and voice tone? Here is a great guideline to live by:

> *...Everyone should be quick to listen, slow to speak*
> *and slow to become angry, for man's anger does not*
> *bring about the righteous life that God desires.*

—James 1:19-20

#3 REMEMBER THE RELATIONSHIP IS GREATER THAN ANY ISSUE

There is one more tendency of the aggressive personality I want to point out. In their zeal to resolve an issue, the aggressive person is prone to become so fixated on solving the problem that they overlook the other person in the process.

Can you identify? If so, I encourage you to learn to put yourself in the other person's shoes as you move through issues. You need to train yourself to go through the person (consider their thoughts, feelings, and perspective) to get to the issue. Also keep in mind that the value of your relationship with them is greater than the issue at hand. Always remember, people are ultimately more important than issues (or at least equally important). If you plow through an issue without considering the people involved, people will likely get blown up in the process.

*Everyone should be quick to listen, slow to speak and
slow to become angry, for man's anger does not bring
about the righteous life that God desires.*

—JAMES 1:19-20

HELPFUL INSIGHTS FOR THE PASSIVE PERSON

#1 DEAL WITH ISSUES TRUTHFULLY

Now for those with a passive personality, you too have some things to recognize and guard against. One such tendency is avoiding issues in order to avoid being hurt or hurting others. If you minimize an important issue or simply pretend it doesn't exist, it will not work itself out or go away. I have been there and done that. It doesn't work. The result of this is that many issues—especially important ones—often go unaddressed.

When we avoid issues, it creates more hostility and distance in our relationships. It also results in a failure to confront others in their wrongdoing and/or sin. In the end, avoidance is actually a lack of true love and grace.

What's the answer? God instructs us in His Word:

*Therefore each of you must put off falsehood and speak
truthfully to his neighbor, for we are all members of one
body.*

—EPHESIANS 4:25

87

And in the same chapter, just nine verses earlier, we are encouraged to...

> ...*Lovingly follow the truth at all times—speaking*
> *truly, dealing truly, living truly—and so become more*
> *and more in every way like Christ who is the Head of*
> *his body, the Church.*

—EPHESIANS 4:15 TLB

If you have the tendency to stuff the truth and avoid dealing with the issues, you will need to proactively work at overcoming these hindrances. You will need to put off whatever is keeping you from openly facing issues and put on the ability to move through conflict.

#2 GUARD AGAINST BEING TOO SENSITIVE

As we have learned, the passive person also has a propensity to being overly sensitive. That is, they make something personal that is not intended to be personal. This is what Tom did in our example in Chapter 4. His wife, Jennifer, made a comment about him not buying the "right" rolls. Tom took her words and turned them into an all-out personal attack, thinking himself a complete failure. This was certainly not Jennifer's intention. She was not focusing on Tom or his capabilities. She was focusing on the rolls (the issue).

Tom, the passive spouse, had a personality weakness of being too sensitive, so he took his wife's comments as a personal attack. At the same time, Jennifer, the aggressive spouse, had a weakness of being too abrupt. Her response, along with a lack of expressed appreciation for what Tom did do, is probably what ultimately set Tom off. This balance and tension of *oversensitivity* and *issue-focused* **insensitivity** is a common dynamic I see in couples with opposite personalities.

If you find yourself as the passive spouse like Tom, I encourage you to learn to depersonalize your mate's responses, even if they are abrupt or harsh. Yes, he or she probably needs to work on how and what they respond. But you can avoid a lot of heartache by simply choosing to believe the best of your spouse and not automatically making negative assumptions regarding their motives. In their heart of hearts, they really do love you. And their opinion does not change your worth and value.

#3 GET THE FACTS RIGHT BEFORE DRAWING CONCLUSIONS

There's one more tendency I believe that needs to be mentioned and it is the inclination to make false assumptions. Passive people are more prone to do this because they are often not openly honest with others. Instead of sharing their own true thoughts and feelings and asking for clarifying information, they are left to their own private interpretations. Unfortunately, they often assume the worst of someone (even their spouse) without first getting the facts straight. They then get angry and offended all because of untrue assumptions.

If you have found yourself jumping to conclusions only to learn they were wrong, here are some words of advice straight from the mouth of God:

> *He who gets wisdom loves his own soul; he who cherishes understanding prospers.*

> **—PROVERBS 19:8**

Make sure you have the facts right before drawing conclusions. This will help you avoid getting upset over something that is not meant or intended.

Those who are passive need to deal with issues truthfully and guard against being too sensitive or jumping to conclusions.

So Ask Yourself...
"Where Do I Fall on the Personality Continuum?"

At this point I must state that it is very important to be genuine and honest with yourself, your spouse, and with God. He will help you to determine accurately where you and your partner fall on the personality continuum, and more importantly, help you get to the root of why you tend to act and react the way you do.

Think for a moment and ask yourself these questions: *Am I more aggressive and controlling, or am I more stable, assertive, and in the middle of the spectrum? Do I feel inwardly compelled to have my own way—as if my security and stability depend on it? Or am I simply trying to ignite a dialogue on issues as they arise? Can I easily let go of an issue and let it be what it is? Or do I feel compelled to fit everything into my "box"?* If you can identify with these characteristics, you may very well be on the aggressive/assertive side of the continuum.

On the other hand, if you are overly sensitive to what goes on around you or you are simply laid-back and don't really care what happens one way or another, you are probably on the passive/laid-back side of the continuum. Ask yourself, *Do I tend to avoid conflict to keep from being hurt and offended? Or am I simply attempting to discern the level of importance of each issue—wanting to overlook the minor things and not make "mountains out of molehills"? Am I indecisive, dependent, and need the input and approval of others? Or am I simply asking for feedback from others to cultivate a healthy negotiation?*

Again, knowing where you and your spouse are on the continuum and why you operate the way you do will greatly diminish the risk of misinterpreting one another and making each other out to be something you are not.

Hopefully, as you and your spouse begin to ask yourselves these kinds of questions and answer honestly, you will begin to see more of who you really are and what makes you tick relationally. With this more accurate assessment, you can both begin to grant each other grace and work together concerning your personalities instead of working against one another.

At this point you may be asking, "How do we navigate all these dynamics in our relationship, Dave? How can we understand the primary needs we each have as individuals and work together to protect, preserve, and meet these needs? How can we understand and navigate the differences in our personalities? More importantly, how can we keep our needs and differences from becoming a wedge that divides us?"

The answers to these and many other questions will come to light in the chapters ahead. But now that we have looked at the "WHY" as to what lies underneath many relational dynamics, let's take a look at God's heart desire for you and your spouse in marriage—the "WHAT" we are striving for in marriage. I call it "The House of Intimacy."

CHAPTER SUMMARY 5

While most operate largely out of either the passive or the aggressive side of the personality continuum, many exhibit a mix of traits from both sides. To a great degree, people and their personalities are primarily shaped by the environment in which they grew up and how their value and security have been influenced. Both those with an aggressive personality and those with a passive personality have certain tendencies they must recognize and guard against. Knowing where you and your spouse are on the continuum and why you operate the way you do will greatly diminish the risk of misinterpreting and hurting one another.

(1) Gary Smalley, *Making Love Last Forever* (Word Publishing, 1996, p. 159). (2) See John 3:16.

Making It Yours ────────────────────────────

1. Think back to your home environment as a child. Did you receive a steady flow of praise and affirmation? Were you criticized, spoken down to, or made to feel worthless? As best you can remember, describe the kinds of words that were spoken to you and the tone / attitude in which they were delivered. Also, how secure did you feel in your home environment? Did you grow up in an abusive or unstable household? Was it a rigid environment, or was there room for personal choice and freedom? **Pause and pray**, asking the Lord to show you how these factors have shaped your personality. Write anything He reveals and ask Him to heal and restore your heart. **The kinds of words/phrases I remember hearing most often included...**

    _____

    _____

    _____

    The sense of stability or instability I experience in my home was...

    _____

    _____

    _____

    I believe God is showing me that this shaped my personality in the following ways:

    _____

    _____

    _____

2. One influence that drives people to the more passive end of the spectrum is an individual's *criteria of worth*. These are

the spoken and unspoken standards that shape our personal belief system as to what makes us have worth and value. Stop and ask yourself: *What was my criterion of worth while growing up? What messages from my peers, parents, the media, and others made me feel I had worth / value?*

My Criteria of Worth While Growing Up Was...

_____

_____

_____

Is this criterion of worth accurate or faulty? Is it *still* your criteria? If not, how has it changed?

_____

_____

_____

3. What is the greatest challenge you see in your personality that you can surrender to the Lord? How would you say this characteristic is impacting your relationships most—especially your marriage? What is the most beneficial adjustment(s) you can personally make to bring about more peace and harmony in your home?

The greatest challenge I see with my personality that I now SURRENDER to God is...

_____

_____

I feel this is impacting my marriage most by...

_____

_____

_____

The most beneficial ADJUSTMENT I believe God is asking me to make with His strength is...

_____

_____

_____

PART II

THE "WHAT" OF A HEALTHY MARRIAGE

DISCOVERING THE IMPORTANCE OF INTIMACY

"God's design for marriage is a sacrificial male leading an honoring female. Their love directed selflessly toward one another was meant to perpetuate their relationship throughout life. God's design for marriage creates a perfect friendship between a man and a woman."

—JIMMY EVANS[1]

CHAPTER 6

THE FOUNDATION OF INTIMACY: BEING PARTNERS AND COMPANIONS

*The Lord God said, "It is not good for the man to
be alone.
I will make a helper suitable for him."*

—Genesis 2:18

Almost every single person I meet has a strong desire to one day get married. Like most of us, they have spent time contemplating and daydreaming about that special someone they will one day meet and with whom they will spend the rest of their lives.

Whether you are married or single, there was probably a time when you reflected on the idea of getting married. You thought about the excitement of entering into a close relationship. You imagined having a person to genuinely love, communicate with, and feel connected to. You dreamed of having someone to hang out with and engage in fun activities. You looked forward to having a person to set goals with, make decisions, and do life together. You may have even envisioned having someone to pray with, worship God, and grow spiritually together. And last, but certainly not least, you were also excited about having someone to be romantically involved with—someone to enjoy being physically connected to.

What do all these aspirations have in common? They all describe the joy of **true intimacy** in marriage. That's what we all desire and dream of having. Indeed, that is what God has always intended for marriage. Ironically, after couples say "I do" and then sadly end up in my office for marriage counseling, issues of intimacy are typically what they are struggling with most.

"I feel so emotionally disconnected," some reveal in frustration. Others report, "For a long time I have felt that we are on completely different Spiritual planes." Most couples inform me that they just can't seem to communicate openly and effectively resolve any issues. It's as though they are living in two different worlds. Many also report that their sexual relations are virtually nonexistent.

Again and again, I hear these kinds of reports. Many are struggling just to be in the same room together. Faced with feelings of loneliness and isolation, men and women who were once excited about being together have become distant, like roommates living under the same roof.

When I ask them what they are looking for, they each paint a similar picture. In so many words, they tell me that what they really want is true intimacy in marriage. The good news is that this is God's original design for us, and if we will humble ourselves and seek Him for wisdom and strength, He will empower us to experience what we long for.

Having a person to genuinely love, communicate with,
and feel connected to is all a part of true intimacy.
This is God's original design for marriage.

Over the years of working with couples, I have developed what I call the **"House of Intimacy."** This model depicts intimacy in marriage from A-Z in three basic levels: 1. the Foundation, 2. the Heart, 3. and the Peak. The **Foundation of Intimacy** is *Being Companions and Partners.* This is our focus for this chapter.

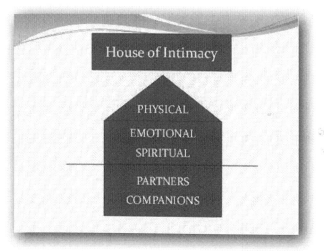

BUILDING A STRONG FOUNDATION
At the foundation of the House of Intimacy are the important elements of *Being Companions and Partners.* Without

maintaining these two fundamental and foundational elements of marriage, your marital "house" is ultimately built on relational sand and it will not endure.

In Genesis 2:18 we read, "The Lord God said, 'It is not good for the man to be alone. I will make a helper suitable for him.'" In this verse we learn that thousands of years ago, God brought the man and woman together and established marriage for two significant reasons. First, He brought man and woman together to combat loneliness and isolation. God brought Eve into Adam's life for him to have a *permanent companion* with whom to share his life. Second, He brought man and woman together so that the man would have a *permanent partner* (a helper) with whom to navigate life. Specifically, God brought Eve into Adam's life to help him in the daily care and oversight of His creation. Companionship and partnership are all about doing life together. Truly, this is the foundation of intimacy.

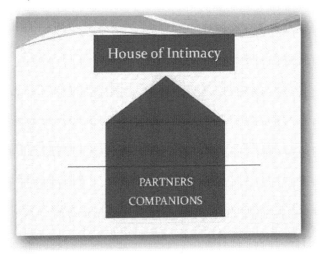

The Foundation of Intimacy is being Companions and Partners—it's doing life together.

What is a Companion?

While on the surface, the words companion and partner seem the same, there is a difference. By definition...

Companionship is *the relationship of friends or companions; fellowship.* Words that convey companionship are company, friendship, camaraderie, and closeness. As a companion of your spouse, you accompany them, living with and serving each other.[2]

WHAT BREAKS DOWN COMPANIONSHIP?

There are three primary causes to consider. The most obvious is a lack of common interests. If this is your situation, I encourage you to be willing to venture into your spouse's world and try something new. This willingness is an expression of humility and true love. It goes a long way to bridge the great divide. When my wife, DeAnn, and I were first married, I would accompany her to quilting shows. While quilting was not my great passion, simply spending time with her was.

Two other significant causes for the breakdown of companionship include letting the busyness of life crowd out "together" time and simply not making companionship a priority. Couples often report to me that over time they simply neglected fostering their own marriage by allowing a preoccupation with kids, busy schedules, and their own agendas get in the way. Can you identify with any of these issues? If so, there are ways to overcome them.

WHAT ACTIVITIES FOSTER COMPANIONSHIP?

Couples that enjoy sweet companionship regularly engage in fun activities together, such as enjoying meaningful conversation, caring mutually for one another, spending quality time as a couple with others, and simply taking pleasure in hanging out together.

As the old saying goes: the couple that *plays* together *stays* together! Contentment in marriage will grow as you share common interests and activities as a couple. Some couples tell me they don't feel like they have much in common as far as interests or hobbies. In actuality, you don't have to have a boatload of common interests. All you need to do is find one or two activities you both enjoy and milk them for all they are worth. What's most important is spending consistent, quality time together. That builds companionship!

As a companion, you accompany your spouse, living with and serving each other as friends.

BALANCING ALONE TIME, TOGETHER TIME, AND TIME WITH OTHERS

Keep in mind that part of building a healthy relationship is having a balance of *alone time, together time,* and *time with others.* **Alone time** is your time of solitude without anyone else around. It is the time you get to spend doing the things you like to do by yourself. Some people get their batteries charged by being alone and need more of it than others. When my wife and I first got married, I was still finishing my graduate degrees. As a result, I was home most evenings. One evening she gently asked me, "Don't you have some place to go or something to do?" It was then I realized that she needed more alone time than I did. Out of respect and care for her, I found something to do.

Together time is time spent *as a couple.* Many couples enjoy going out to dinner together. Others will take in a new movie or read a book together. Still others enjoy a good hike or quiet walk along the beach or lake. There is really no limit to what you can do. All that matters is that it's the two of you…together.

Together time can also be experienced *as a family.* When my kids were younger one of our favorite "together times" as a family was movie night. On Saturday evenings we would pop popcorn, crank up the surround sound, and take in a good flick together. Shared experiences like these can create a real openness and connectedness between family members that is truly life-giving.

With-others time is time you spend with other couples, families, or on a girl or guy's night out. I believe periodic times of female and male bonding is important, and I really look forward to and cherish them. Time with others can enrich us greatly as individuals and couples, providing all who participate with new insights, wisdom, direction, and encouragement. God's Word declares, "As iron sharpens iron, so a friend sharpens a friend" (Proverbs 27:17 NLT).

Again, balance is the key. Stop and think: *How is my leisure time divided up? What percentage of time do I spend alone, together with my spouse, and with others?* Taking it a step further, what percentage of time would you personally prefer to spend in each of these categories? What do you believe is healthy for your marriage? This is an exercise I sometimes give the couples with whom I work. My goal is to see how well you and your spouse know one another and to determine if you are on the same page relationally.

Part of building a healthy relationship is having a balance of alone time, together time, and time with others.

One couple I worked with several years ago gave me the following percentages. He said, "I would like 90 percent *alone* time, 10 percent *together* time, and 0 percent *others* time." No joke! That was his answer. He was a computer junkie and liked to stay in his room playing computer games and surfing the net. His wife, on the other hand, replied, "I would like 10 percent *alone* time, 90 percent *together* time, and 0 percent *others* time." To this I responded to them, "That is exactly why the two of you are in my office."

Thankfully, I was able to help them come up with more reasonable percentages for each category. I then gave them the assignment of putting some specific activities down for each time segment. At their next appointment they reported that they had made progress and felt closer as a couple. Clearly, their previous approach was never going to cultivate good companionship, and the same is true for you and your spouse.

So, an important question you need to ask and answer is: *How much time are we spending together as a couple?* Even if you have younger children, it is vital to take time for just the two of you. This is typically not going to just "happen." You need to intentionally make it a priority. Plan for specific times together and write them down on the calendar. Remember, **we find a way to make time for the things we value the most**.

To help you build companionship in your marriage, I suggest you try to go out at least once or twice a month—just the two of you. Go out to dinner, to a movie, or for a walk in the park. Explore new adventures together and key in on what you like to do for fun as a couple. If for some reason you can't get out of the house, plan a "house date." Get a good movie for your kids along with some snacks they like, and then you and your spouse eat dinner together or just sit and talk.

I probably don't need to convince you that your intimacy as a couple will eventually suffer if you are not spending time together to cultivate it. You need to learn the expectations that you and your mate have for spending time together and be willing to adjust them to reach an agreeable compromise. Coming to this understanding will move you forward toward greater intimacy.

It is vital that you intentionally take time for just the two of you. It's not going to just "happen." You must make it a priority.

WHAT IS A PARTNER?

Now that we have a better perspective on being a companion, let's take a look at what it means to be a partner. By definition...

> **Partnership** is *an arrangement in which parties agree to cooperate to advance their mutual interests.* Merriam Webster expands this definition, describing partnership as *one associating with another especially in an action.*[3] Other words that convey the meaning of partnership include collaboration, joint venture, alliance, union, and team.

While the word companion serves to describe what the relationship *is,* partnership explains what the relationship *does.* It is more action-oriented.

WHAT CAUSES A BREAKDOWN IN PARTNERSHIP?

There are five to consider. One of the biggest reasons is not taking time to discuss and work through issues together. Every decision you and your spouse work out as "a team" will help build a sense of partnership in your marriage. Every decision you make individually will only serve to undermine your union. A second cause of breakdown is when issues are discussed but there is an inability (or unwillingness) to negotiate and reach a compromise. It is important to learn to compromise and look for mutually beneficial solutions to foster a sense of togetherness.

Right on the heels of a lack of compromise is when one person in the relationship dominates and makes all the decisions. This practice only serves to diminish a true sense of partnership. Two other causes for a breakdown in partnership include one person bearing the bulk of all the responsibilities as well as not looking out for or helping each other. The one who bears the bulk of the household tasks will not feel as if they are experiencing a partnership in marriage. It is essential to look proactively for ways to lighten each other's load, particularly when you have small children.

HOW CAN YOU PROMOTE PARTNERSHIP?

You may begin promoting a partnership by simply making important decisions together. As I mentioned earlier, I tell couples that every decision they make together fosters unity, while every decision they make separately encourages disunity. Another key to building a partnership is to proactively set future goals together for your marriage and family. Most couples report that they have never really sat down and discussed any goals together. A third way to foster a partnership is to simply accomplish something together as a couple. Complete a project together or join a sports team. Another significant way to build a partnership is in learning to negotiate and come to a mutual compromise on the daily matters of life. We will discuss negotiation in greater detail in Chapter 10.

A genuine sense of partnership is also cultivated by simply navigating the daily ebb and flow of life and operating as a team. As you and your spouse support, care for, and minister to one another's needs, you will grow closer together and experience partnership the way God intended. Through the apostle Paul, He says,

> *...Make me truly happy by loving each other and agreeing wholeheartedly with each other, **working together** with one heart and mind and purpose. Don't be*

selfish; don't live to make a good impression on others.
Be humble, thinking of others as better than yourself.

—Philippians 2:2-3 TLB

God also gives us a great description of what it means to be good partners in marriage through King Solomon. Late in his life, this man of unequaled wisdom looked back on the many relationships he had experienced and spoke truth that transcends all generations:

> *Two are better than one, because they have a good*
> *return for their work: If one falls down, his friend can*
> *help him up. But pity the man who falls and has no*
> *one to help him up! Also, if two lie down together, they*
> *will keep warm. But how can one keep warm alone?*
> *Though one may be overpowered, two can defend them-*
> *selves. A cord of three strands is not quickly broken.*

—Ecclesiastes 4:9-12

These verses describe a couple who has a strong partnership in marriage. They encourage and lift one another up. They fend for each other and mutually support one another's best interests. Clearly, we get the sense that they are on the same page of life, carrying out God's divine design to be each other's helpers.

As a partner, you and your spouse agree to take
action and work together to advance your mutual
interests.

DO YOU FEEL YOUR MARRIAGE IS A TRUE PARTNERSHIP?

So how would you describe your marital partnership? Are you navigating life together and engaging with your spouse, or is one or both of you simply going about doing your own thing? Bill, in our first marital scenario from Chapter 1, was doing his own thing. He was always focused on his agenda, leaving Jen behind to fend for herself. The result was no true partnership.

How about making decisions and setting goals? Do you make them together, or does one of you tend to be the dominant "boss" of the relationship? Remember John and Sally from our marital scenarios in Chapter 1? John felt his wife was very controlling and that she wanted to make all the decisions around the house and in their marriage. In fact, he often stated that he felt like a "puppet on strings" in his own home. Obviously, John didn't feel that he and Sally had a true partnership. As a result, he felt more and more defeated and became relationally disconnected from her.

How about teamwork? Are you and your spouse helping each other in the daily grind of life, or does one of you tend to bear the brunt of the workload? When I talk with women who work outside the home, they often tell me they feel as if they have two full-time jobs. One job is at work and the other at home. Consequently, they are constantly worn out. Even women who don't work outside the home have expressed feeling as if they work twenty-four hours a day, seven days a week trying to keep their house and family together.

In order to foster a true sense of "togetherness," it is important to work graciously at lightening each other's load. What amazes me is that this is what we did naturally while we were dating. "What can I do for you? How can I serve you and make your life better?" was our unspoken heart's cry. Then somehow after we got married, our motto quickly became, "Ok, now what are you going to do for me? How are you going to serve me and complete my life?"

As you live life as a married couple, don't throw your sense of *servanthood* out the window and replace it and with a sense of "self-ish-hood." Look for ways to minister to and care for your spouse. This is vital to building and maintaining a genuine partnership in marriage and crucial to developing intimacy. It will keep you from building resentment and emotional distance towards one another.

I encourage you to take time to sit with your spouse and discuss what a marital companionship and partnership mean to each of you. Read through and answer the questions together at the end of this chapter. In what practical ways can you work together to experience this in your relationship? How much sweeter would it be for the two of you to "do life together?"

Chapter Summary 6

True intimacy is what we all desire deep in our hearts. It's what God has always intended for marriage. The Foundation of Intimacy is being *companions* and *partners*—it's doing life together. As a *companion*, you accompany your spouse, living with, playing with, and serving each other as friends. As a *partner*, you and your spouse agree to take action and work together to glorify God and advance your mutual interests. To build a healthy relationship, there must be a balance of *alone time*, *together time*, and *time with others.*

(1) Jimmy Evans, *Marriage on the Rock* (Dallas, TX: Marriage Today, 2012, p. 89). (2) Adapted from the definition of *Companion* (http://www.merriam-webster.com/dictionary/companion, accessed 2/11/16). (3) Adapted from the definition of *Partner* (http://www.merriam-webster.com/dictionary/partner, accessed 2/11/16).

Making It Yours ————————————————————————————

1. Carefully reread the definitions of *Companion* and *Partner.* In what specific ways do you see you and your spouse functioning as a true companions and true partners? What practical steps can you take to improve the level of companionship and partnership you are both experiencing?
   The ways in which my spouse and I are operating as TRUE COMPANIONS include...

   ————————————————————————————

   ————————————————————————————

   ————————————————————————————

   The ways in which my spouse and I are operating as TRUE PARTNERS include...

   ————————————————————————————

   ————————————————————————————

   ————————————————————————————

   With God's help, the steps I can take to IMPROVE our level of companionship and partnership are...

   ————————————————————————————

   ————————————————————————————

   ————————————————————————————

2. One of the most common causes for a breakdown in companionship is a lack of common interests. Stop and think: What are the top ten things your spouse enjoys doing? What are the top ten things you enjoy doing? What are three interests that you share? Name three things your spouse enjoys that you are willing to try to build your companionship.
   THE TOP TEN THINGS MY SPOUSE ENJOYS:

   ————————————————————————————

   ————————————————————————————

THE TOP TEN THINGS I ENJOY:

_____

_____

THE INTERESTS WE SHARE ARE:

_____

_____

THREE THINGS I AM WILLING TO TRY TO BUILD COMPANIONSHIP ARE:

_____

_____

3. How is your leisure time divided up? What percentage of time do you spend *alone, together* with your spouse, and *with others*? What percentage of time would you personally prefer to spend in each of these categories?
   Presently, our percentage of *alone* time, *together* time, and time *with others* is as follows:

   _____

   _____

   My *personal preference* of how we invest our times in these categories is...

   _____

   _____

4. Have you lost your sense of *servanthood* and replaced it with a sense of "selfish-hood"? It can happen to the best of us, but with God's help we can make some changes and begin to experience the love we had with our spouse when we first met. *Pause and pray.* Ask God to remind you of the things you did when you first met your spouse that he/she liked. Also, ask Him to show you practical ways you can be a blessing to them on a daily basis.

The things my spouse loved when we were dating that I will do again by God's grace include...

_____

_____

_____

With God's strength, *I will be mindful to be a blessing* to my spouse each day by doing...

_____

_____

_____

(For help, check out Revelation 2:4-5 and Galatians 6:9-10).

"The highest or deepest level of relationship is the spiritual level. …Fellowship around the Word and prayer will develop the deepest level of intimacy between individuals because it is a spiritual connection."

—JOHN BEVERE[1]

CHAPTER 7

THE HEART OF INTIMACY: SPIRITUAL AND EMOTIONAL ONENESS

*For this reason a man will leave his father
and mother and be united to his wife,
and they will become one flesh.*

—GENESIS 2:24

NOW THAT WE know and have a better understanding of the Foundation of Intimacy, *Being Companions and Partners*, let's take some time to focus on the **Heart of Intimacy**, which is *Spiritual and Emotional Oneness.*

While it is one thing to be your spouse's companion and go to a movie and share popcorn, it is quite another to pray together, engage with God together, and share the true thoughts and feelings of your heart and soul. There is a greater sense of vulnerability. Yet while the risk of rejection is greater, there is also a greater opportunity for connection—a chance to experience oneness beyond your greatest expectations. It is on this level that your whole house of intimacy is most greatly impacted.

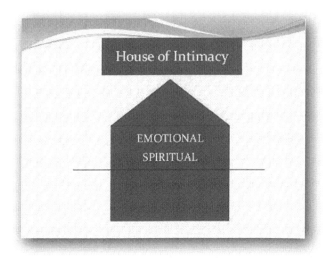

Spiritual and emotional oneness create the overall connection, or disconnection, a couple experiences in marriage. It is at this level that husbands and wives who come in for counseling typically struggle with most. Many have shared with me that they have a good foundation of companionship and partnership in marriage. They spend adequate time together and excel at making life work as a team. However, they do not feel spiritually or emotionally connected.

Whenever I hear a spouse say, "I love him/her, but I'm not 'in love' with him/her," what they are essentially telling me is that they don't feel a spiritual or emotional connection with their spouse. If this is something you have experienced from time to time, there is definitely hope to rebuild your spiritual and emotional connection.

The Heart of Intimacy is Spiritual and Emotional
Oneness—the level on which your house of intimacy is
most greatly impacted.

THE CORE ELEMENTS OF SPIRITUAL AND EMOTIONAL ONENESS

WHAT IS SPIRITUAL ONENESS?

In my denomination, we hold to the Westminster Confession of Faith, which is a book that explains the systematic doctrines of the Bible and matters of faith. Included in it is a set of catechism questions, which are clear statements in a question-and-answer format of what we believe that describe the essentials of the Christian faith.

The first question of the Shorter Catechism[2] reads,

Q: What is the chief end of man?

In other words, what is man's ultimate goal and purpose in life? The answer is,

A: To glorify God and enjoy Him forever.

I believe this is a great summary that captures the essence of spiritual oneness in marriage. The couple who regularly walks with God, enjoys God, and brings Him glory together will experience the greatest level of spiritual oneness.

Activities that foster spiritual oneness include:

- Worshiping together
- Praying together
- Spending time in God's Word together (and individually)
- Talking about God together
- Fellowshipping with other believers
- Engaging in some sort of service or ministry together

What causes a breakdown in spiritual oneness in marriage? The answer is doing *none* of the above together as a married couple. Another major deterrent to spiritual unity is continuously being on different spiritual levels. One may have a serious sense of wanting to walk with God and know Him better, while the other is not so earnest about their faith. Over time this will cause a serious feeling of spiritual disunity in the marriage.

In Deuteronomy 6:4-13, we are given a great description of spiritual oneness in marriage and in the family. Devoted followers of God of Hebrew descent in both Old Testament times and today refer to this portion of Scripture as the *Shema*. It is the most important part of their prayers and serves as the centerpiece of the morning and evening devotions every day. In these verses we read,

Hear, O Israel: The Lord our God, the Lord is one. Love the Lord your God with all your heart and with all your soul and with all your strength.

These commandments that I give you today are to be upon your hearts. Impress them on your children. Talk about them when you sit at home and when you walk along the road, when you lie down and when you get up. Tie them as symbols on your hands and bind them on your foreheads. Write them on the doorframes of your houses and on your gates.

When the Lord your God brings you into the land he swore to your fathers, to Abraham, Isaac and Jacob, to give you—a land with large, flourishing cities you did not build, houses filled with all kinds of good things you did not provide, wells you did not dig, and vineyards and olive groves you did not plant— then when you eat and are satisfied, be careful that you do not

*forget the Lord, who brought you out of Egypt, out of the land of
slavery. Fear the Lord your God, serve him only....*

In essence, these verses tell us that spiritual oneness is keeping
God at the very center of your marriage and family. As you and
your spouse worship together, talk openly about God and His
Word, and make Him the major frame of reference for your
marriage and family, you will experience the joys of spiritual
oneness.

---

*The couple who regularly walks with God, enjoys God,
and brings Him glory together will experience the
greatest level of spiritual oneness.*

OBSTACLES TO SPIRITUAL ONENESS

For some couples, connecting spiritually is a challenge. When I
inquire about a couple's spiritual harmony, one of the greatest
responses I get is the issue of *time.*

"Life is just too chaotic to fit everything in," they respond.
"Between our work schedules, our kids' activities, keeping the
house straight, and all of life's other demands, it is a challenge
to find time to connect spiritually."

I understand how "full" life can be. But remember, we *make*
time for the things that matter most to us. In light of all that I
have experienced in my personal life as well as in working with
others, I can say that **spending time with God together as a**

married couple is far more important than all the things that keep us from spending that time.

Another common reason I hear from one or both partners who can't seem to connect spiritually is that they struggle with feelings of *awkwardness* or *inadequacy*. "I just don't feel capable, comfortable, or competent to delve into spiritual matters," one or both spouses will say.

If this describes your situation, I encourage you not to worry about being perfect in your approach to God. Instead of trying to create flawless encounters with Him, simply seek Him and engage with Him together on some attainable level. He promises in His Word,

> *"In those days when you pray, I will listen. If you look for me wholeheartedly, you will find me. I will be found by you," says the LORD....*

—JEREMIAH 29:12-14 NLT

So keep things light and enjoyable. Seek the Lord together with your spouse in simplicity and sincerity. In the end, that's what matters most.

WHERE ARE YOU AND YOUR SPOUSE?

Here are some simple questions to ask yourself and your spouse to determine whether or not you are connecting spiritually. First, "Do we feel we're walking with and glorifying God together?" Second, "Are we enjoying God together?" Third, "How much time are we spending together spiritually as a couple and as a family?" Moreover, "Are we worshiping together on a regular basis? Are we in some sort of Bible study as a couple or individually?" Lastly, "Are we engaging in fellowship with other believers?"

Keep in mind that cultivating spiritual oneness should not be a legalistic "ought to" or "have to" activity. Spiritual oneness grows naturally out of a genuine desire and longing to be closer to God and each other. The more time you spend together engaging in spiritual activities, the more you will feel spiritually connected as a couple and as a family.

Now you may be thinking, *Dave, how can my spouse and I practically apply this in our lives?* I suggest you begin by joining together in something simple like reading a good spiritually-based book or a book in the Bible that you are both interested in. Another idea is to join a Bible study as a couple. This will get you out of the house and help you engage spiritually as a couple.

One other great thing to do is to simply begin praying together. Your prayers don't have to be long or elaborate. Just get together for a few minutes each day and thank God for His blessings and tell Him about what is on your heart and mind. You might be surprised at what transpires. It is often amazing what flows out of my client's when we pray together during a counseling session.

---

*Spiritual oneness grows naturally out of a genuine
desire and longing to be closer to God and each other.*

WHAT IS EMOTIONAL ONENESS?

The essence of emotional oneness is **maintaining a strong emotional connection** with your spouse. Emotional oneness is accomplished primarily through, 1. being authentic and transparent, 2. consistently resolving conflict, and 3. treating each other with love and respect.

When a couple informs me that they are struggling in their sexual relationship, there is typically an emotional disconnection at the root of it. A couple's emotional and physical oneness is closely intertwined.

Few things warm my heart more than to see an elderly couple walking together holding hands. It is a sign that they have a strong bond and emotional connection as a couple. On the other hand, a sight that breaks my heart is seeing a couple tense, short-tempered, and critical of one another. This signifies a major emotional breakdown in the marriage relationship.

One of the most crucial elements of emotional oneness is **maintaining peace and harmony** within the relationship. This is largely accomplished through consistently resolving and reconciling over conflict. Keeping your hearts free and clear of hurt, resentment, and bitterness is essential to maintaining an emotional connection. God instructs us through the apostle Paul,

In your anger do not sin: Do not let the sun go down while you are still angry, and do not give the devil a foothold.

—Ephesians 4:26-27

Here God is urging us to resolve our differences quickly and keep short accounts. If we don't, we give the enemy of our soul an opportunity to drive a wedge between us and our spouse and anyone else with whom we are unwilling to make peace.

Several years ago I was working with a new couple who had been referred to me. When they came for their first appointment, I could cut the atmosphere in my office with a knife. The tension was extremely thick. In fact, I had never seen such bitterness and resentment stored up in a couple. It was obvious that they had both let many suns go down on their anger, and there was very little peace or harmony in their relationship.

If this describes your marriage, there is hope! There are significant ways to reconnect emotionally and nurture true love.

Don't give the enemy an inch. Resolve your differences quickly and keep short accounts.

MORE DETAIL ON THE THREE ESSENTIALS TO BUILDING EMOTIONAL ONENESS IN YOUR MARRIAGE

The pathway to establishing and maintaining a strong, healthy emotional bond in your relationship can be achieved by following three basic keys:

#1 - BE TRANSPARENT

The first key is to cultivate the freedom and ability to *be transparent* and vulnerable with one another. We all need to be real and feel safe to share our thoughts and emotions. Otherwise, we will be perpetually living life on the surface and in the mundane.

The more superficial our relationship is, the less emotionally connected we will feel.

It is vital for you and your spouse to be able to share your heart and inner world openly with one another. If your marriage tends to be shallow, the question is why?

There are typically several underlying reasons for shallowness. One common reason is that one or both of you feel awkward at sharing your innermost thoughts. Maybe you or your spouse grew up in a home where personal thoughts, feelings, and experiences were never expressed. Therefore, you never learned to flex your "transparency" muscle.

Another reason for a shallow existence is fear. Often one partner is afraid that if they share their deepest feelings, they will be laughed at, corrected, or minimized. They think it may be too risky to share what is really going on below the surface. Whatever the case may be, these barriers must be removed if a deeper intimacy is to be achieved.

#2 – RESOLVE CONFLICT

Resolving conflict is *maintaining peace*. This is another key to maintaining emotional connectedness. By consistently dealing with and working through conflicts as they arise, you and your spouse can keep your hearts free and clear and remain connected in your relationship. Avoiding conflict and sweeping it under the rug *never* works. Realize that every disagreement you mishandle or choose to ignore becomes another brick in the wall of hostility and resentment that will eventually separate you and your spouse. Left unchecked, this wall can become a great barrier of bitterness.

Are you beginning to see why God urges us not to let the sun go down while we are holding onto anger? This prevents emotional distance from building between us. True, it's not always easy to deal with disagreements that arise. But if we will learn to humble ourselves, turn to God in prayer, and ask Him for the strength to get out of our self-protective comfort zone, He will faithfully provide it. His Word declares, "He gives us more and more strength to stand against all such evil longings." As the Scripture says, "God gives strength to the humble but sets himself against the proud and haughty" (James 4:6 TLB). So get the issues out on the table and resolve them as they take place.

In the upcoming chapters, I will give you some helpful tools to empower you to deal successfully with the issues and differences that arise in your marriage. These tools include communication, negotiation, and reconciliation. However, if avoiding conflict is so substantial that it has become the norm in your life, you may need to consider professional help and guidance in dealing with the underlying problems. A good counselor will help expose and deal with the root issues that are hindering you from getting things out on the table, resolving them, and keeping your hearts free and clear toward one another.

Learn to humble yourself and turn to God in prayer.
He will provide the strength you need to pursue peace
with your spouse and others if you ask Him.

#3 – TREAT EACH OTHER WITH LOVE AND RESPECT

How you and I treat one another on a daily basis is a third key to maintaining emotional connectedness. Stop and think: Are you and your spouse kind and supportive of each other, or are you mean and critical? Are you patient or are you short and irritated? Do you speak in ways that build one another up, or are you verbally tearing each other down?

It's no coincidence that God specifically instructs us to "encourage each other and build each other up..." (1 Thessalonians 5:11 NLT). He also urges us to "get rid of all bitterness, rage, anger, harsh words, and slander, as well as all types of evil behavior. Instead, be kind to each other, tender-hearted, forgiving one another, just as God through Christ has forgiven you" (Ephesians 4:31-32 NLT).

Simple kindness and words of encouragement go a long way in building and maintaining a healthy emotional connection. In Proverbs 12:25 we learn that "an anxious heart weighs a man down, but a kind *word* cheers him up." And in Proverbs 25:11 we read, "A *word* aptly spoken is like apples of gold in settings of silver." These truly are great words of wisdom.

For me, it would be very difficult to be married to a mean, angry, and critical person. Thankfully, that is not the case. While I don't need a lot of positive affirmation, I would rather hear nothing at all than to hear negativity only.

WHERE ARE YOU AND YOUR SPOUSE?

Are you connecting emotionally? Here are some simple questions to ask yourself and your spouse. First, "Do we have a deep relationship or is our marriage shallow?" Second, "Are we able to talk on deep levels, or do we find ourselves communicating mainly about the weather, sports, and our kids' activities?" Answers to these questions will help you know if you and your spouse are struggling with transparency.

Next, how are you at resolving conflict? To determine this, ask yourself and your spouse, "Are we resolving disagreements and settling our differences, or are we sweeping matters under the rug?" If the latter is true, what is keeping the two of you from getting issues out in the open? Is it awkwardness? Is it fear? Or is it something else?

Lastly, are you and your spouse supportive and encouraging of one another, or are you largely ignoring each other's emotional and physical needs?

Simple kindness and words of encouragement go a long way in building and maintaining a healthy emotional connection.

The good news is, wherever you and your spouse are, you can work at improving any of these areas in your marriage. The key is to do something about it proactively and not settle for less. For starters, I suggest taking the time to do one kind thing for your spouse each day. This might be offering a word of encouragement, performing a task to lighten their load, or giving a small token of appreciation in the form of a note or gift.

You might also consider sitting down together and answering how you feel you are doing in the areas of transparency, resolving conflict, and treating each other with love and respect. Again, if you are really struggling to connect, you may need to get together with a counselor or professional to get to the root issues and sort things out.

CHAPTER SUMMARY 7

The Heart of Intimacy is Spiritual and Emotional Oneness. The couple who regularly walks with God, enjoys God, and brings Him glory together will experience the greatest level of spiritual oneness. This is accomplished by keeping God at the center of your marriage and family. Emotional oneness is attained by being authentic and transparent, resolving conflict quickly, and treating each other with love and respect. The more time you spend together engaging in spiritual activities and sharing your innermost thoughts and feelings, the more spiritually and emotionally connected you will feel as a couple.

(1) John Bevere, *The Holy Spirit, An Introduction* (Palmer Lake, CO: Messenger International, 2013, p. 91). (2) What is the *Shorter Catechism?* (http://www.westminsterconfession.org/confessional-standards/the-westminster-shorter-catechism.php, accessed 2/18/16).

Making It Yours ————————————————————————

1. Would you say that you are experiencing *spiritual oneness* with your mate? Take time to reread the list of activities that foster spiritual oneness. Which activities are you presently engaged in? What might you and your mate do to connect more closely with God and, consequently, each other?

    ————————————————————————————

    ————————————————————————————

    The activities my spouse and I are engaged in that promote spiritual oneness include:

    ————————————————————————————

    ————————————————————————————

    Some things I can do to help my spouse and me to connect more closely to God are:

    ————————————————————————————

    ————————————————————————————

2. Are you and your spouse *emotionally connected*? Read through this brief evaluation and answer each question as honestly as you can.

    Using the numbers **1** through **5**, place a number in the space next to each question that best answers it.

    (Number **1** = Never; **2** = Seldom; **3** = Sometimes; **4** = Often; **5** = Always)

    _____I feel free and safe to share my innermost thoughts and feelings with my spouse.

    _____My spouse and I quickly move to resolve conflicts that arise between us.

_____ I feel a genuine sense of peace and harmony with my spouse.

_____ My spouse and I are supportive and encourage one another.

_____ We willingly meet each other's needs with no strings attached.

Now add up the numbers. If you scored between 20 and 25, you and your spouse are emotionally connected. If you scored between 10 and 15, you are somewhat connected to your mate but have room for improvement. If you scored between 5 and 10, you and your spouse are primarily disconnected. Pause and pray, asking God to reveal anything you need to see about yourself and Him.

Some things I can do to improve my emotional connection with my spouse include:

_____

_____

_____

3. Whether you need help resolving conflict, being transparent, or connecting spiritually, God is ready, willing, and able to help! Check out these promises He made to you in His Word. Write what He reveals to you as you carefully read each one.

James 1:5; Psalm 25:8-9; 32:8

_____

_____

Isaiah 40:28-29; 41:10, 13; Hebrews 13:5-6

_____

_____

"We have been set free to experience the joy of our sexuality. We have also been given the resources we need to help us undo the distortions of our sexuality that inevitably will follow from our brokenness and imperfections as humans. This healing is built into God's plan for all humanity. All it takes from us is some cooperation with this plan."

—Dr. Archibald D. Hart[1]

CHAPTER 8

THE PEAK OF INTIMACY: PHYSICAL ONENESS

The man and his wife were both naked, and they felt no shame.

—GENESIS 2:25

HOPEFULLY IT IS becoming clear that building and maintaining your House of Intimacy is a vital part of experiencing a fulfilling marriage. As we have learned, this begins with cultivating a healthy Companionship and Partnership—*the Foundation of Intimacy*. It continues and is strengthened by developing and maintaining Spiritual and Emotional Oneness—*the Heart of Intimacy*. With these aspects in place, Physical Oneness—*the Peak of Intimacy*—can more readily be experienced.

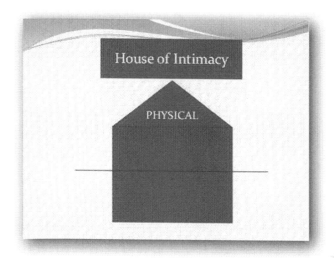

This is the top of our house—the culmination, or peak, of close intimacy. Typically, if the rest of the house is in order, the physical relationship will naturally follow. When a couple is enjoying sweet companionship, charting life together as partners, maintaining an emotional connection, and walking with God and enjoying Him together, they also enjoy a fulfilling physical relationship.

Physical oneness includes:

- holding hands
- hugs
- kisses
- non-sexual touch
- and the sexual relationship

The sexual relationship in marriage is what makes it unique to all other relationships. You will likely experience some sense of intimacy in all other associations in your life, but not to the extent of what you experience in marriage.

I had several friends while growing up and each was a unique relational experience. With one friend in particular, I remember being very close. We played softball and tennis together regularly and then would sit at the end of my driveway sipping iced tea into the wee hours of the morning. We dialogued about life, laughed a lot, and had many deep discussions about God and religion. We definitely had a sense of emotional connection with each other. However, there was no physical aspect to our relationship. It was strictly a friendship-based intimacy.

In marriage, on the other hand, we connect with our spouse on a deeper emotional and physical level than in any other relationship. I believe this is why couples often inform me that they struggle in areas of their marriage that they have no issues with in any other relationship. The deep emotional and physical bond of marriage, coupled with the element of living under the same roof, makes the relationship close and intense. While it can be the most challenging, it can also be the most rewarding.

The sexual relationship in marriage is what makes it unique to all other relationships. It is the peak of the House of Intimacy.

A Marriage Built on Sex Alone Is Unstable

Every once in a while I run into what I call a "canopy couple." This is a husband and a wife who have great sex but everything else in their house is a mess. Day in and day out, they fight like cats and dogs. They can't agree on much of anything. Their communication and conflict-resolution skills are minimal at best, and emotionally and spiritually they are disconnected. Essentially, there is no sense of togetherness in their marriage whatsoever.

Several years ago, I was working with a couple who came into one of our sessions with big smiles on their faces. Excitedly, I asked them what had transpired during the week to produce such euphoria. To my amazement, they said, "Well, we got into a fistfight and really worked some things out." Strangely, this same couple continued to report that their physical relationship was fine. Although this dynamic occurs on some occasions, it is certainly not the norm.

Typically, if a couple is experiencing a strong physical/sexual relationship, they are investing time and effort building up every other area of their House of Intimacy. The greater the stability in the rest of the house, the more enjoyable and healthy their physical relationship will be. While some clients tell me that their sexual relationship is the glue that holds their marital house together, history proves that it is only a matter of time before their house begins to fall apart.

When it comes to marital oneness, I tell couples that spiritual oneness is actually the "glue" that holds a marriage together. That is, each partner's personal relationship with God, their commitment to God and honoring Him with their life, their level of spiritual maturity, and their commitment to their marital vows. While spiritual oneness is the glue that holds a marriage together, it is emotional oneness that is the "driver" of the marriage. The emotional connection or disconnection a couple experiences dictates the condition of the rest of their house from the foundation of companionship all the way up to the physical relationship. In the end, both spiritual and emotional oneness together is the most crucial element in the house. As you and your spouse invest time and energy building your "Heart" of Intimacy, you will begin to experience the rewards of a richer physical relationship.

The true glue that bonds a husband and wife together
as one is spiritual and emotional oneness.

How Can You Rekindle a Fresh Fire of Physical Intimacy?

The truth is God wants you and your spouse to enjoy each other fully in marriage, and this includes sexual intimacy. His Word declares, "God created human beings in his own image. In the image of God he created them; *male* and *female* he created them. Then *God blessed them* and said, 'Be fruitful and multiply...'" (Genesis 1:27-28 NLT). Here we clearly see that God created our sexual identity and our sexual union and He blessed it! Immediately after this, just two verses later, we read, "God saw all that he had made, and it was *very good...*" (Genesis 1:31). When we follow God's plan, our lives are blessed—including our sex life. And there is no shame or embarrassment that comes with it (see Genesis 2:25).

If your sexual relationship is on the rocks, don't be discouraged. There is hope. You can rekindle a fresh fire between you and your spouse by rebuilding your House of Intimacy from the ground level up. Take the steps necessary to reconnect with him or her as friends. True companionship and a mutual partnership is your rock-solid foundation. It will pave the way for developing spiritual and emotional oneness, which in turn will foster physical intimacy in your relationship. If for some reason your marriage seems unable to sustain this, I suggest starting off with simple hugs, kisses, and non-sexual touch. This will get the ball rolling in the right direction.

Keep in mind that no one has a "perfect" House of Intimacy. We are all fallen creatures living in a fallen world. Consequently, our ability to connect intimately in marriage will undoubtedly be affected in some way, shape, or form. It should also be noted that having a perfect House of Intimacy is not the end-all of marriage anyway. Developing and maintaining a spiritually healthy, God-honoring marriage is. The more you and your spouse grow in your relationship with God, the more you will grow together as a couple. Ultimately, marriage must be established on mutual commitment and grace, as we will see more clearly in our final chapter.

To rekindle a fresh fire of physical intimacy with your spouse, take the needed steps to reconnect as friends and develop emotional and spiritual oneness.

A Few Final Thoughts

I often tell couples who come into my office for counseling, "Let's face it. If you were enjoying each other's company and hanging out together...if you felt like you were true partners in caring and looking out for one another, successfully charting life as a team...if you felt like you were walking with God together and enjoying Him as a couple...if you had a strong emotional connection with one another and you were having great sex, you would *not* be in my office right now. You would be somewhere else."

The truth of the matter is that at any given time, one of three things is happening in your relationship: you and your spouse are either *building* your House of Intimacy, *tearing it down*, or *becoming stagnant*. While there are other issues you may need to work through, building and maintaining your House of Intimacy is of prime importance.

The better you understand each of these elements and work at building your "house," the more solid your marriage will be. The key is in knowing the condition of each element. Even more important is in knowing and understanding the areas in which you may struggle, why there is a breakdown, and how to get things successfully back on track.

For additional reading on the topic of physical oneness in marriage, you may want to check out these resources: *Sheet Music: Uncovering the Secrets of Sexual Intimacy* and *Sex Begins in the Kitchen: Creating Intimacy to Make Your Marriage Sizzle* by Kevin Leman. *Intended for Pleasure* by Ed Wheat, M.D. is another consideration.

Chapter Summary 8
The sexual relationship in marriage is what makes it unique to all other relationships. It is the peak of the House of Intimacy. Realize that no one has a "perfect" house. The goal is to develop and maintain a spiritually healthy, God-honoring marriage. To rekindle a fresh fire of physical intimacy with your spouse, take the needed steps to reconnect as friends and develop emotional

and spiritual oneness. The more you and your spouse grow in your relationship with God, the more you will grow together as a couple.

(1) Dr. Archibald D. Hart, *The Sexual Man* (W. Publishing Group, A Division of Thomas Nelson, Inc., Inc., 1994, p. 208).

Making It Yours ──────────────────────────────

1. How would you describe the present condition of your *physical relationship* with your spouse? In light of your answer, how would you describe the other two levels of your House of Intimacy? Are you connecting as *companions* and *partners*? Are you experiencing *spiritual* and *emotional* oneness?
   The Condition of Our *Physical Relationship*:

   _____

   _____

   _____

   The Quality of Our *Companionship* and *Partnership*:

   _____

   _____

   _____

   The Description of Our *Spiritual* and *Emotional Oneness*:

   _____

   _____

   _____

2. Whether your sexual relationship is on the rocks or you and your spouse seem to be doing just fine physically, there is always room for improvement. In what practical ways can you invest in your spouse and marriage to experience a more fulfilling physical oneness? What do you sense God is prompting you to do?

   _____

   _____

   _____

   _____

3. Once you have recorded your answers, sit with your spouse and read through the questions together. Allow him/her to

answer the questions. In what ways have you answered similarly? How have you answered differently? What can the two of you do together to improve your overall House of Intimacy?

_____

_____

_____

_____

PART III

THE "HOW" STEPS TO BRING ABOUT CHANGE

IMPLEMENTING THE TOOLS OF SUCCESS

"In order to communicate more effectively with your partner, you first have to slow down. Good communication takes time. ...When we slow down the conversation with our partner, we are less likely to give hasty orders and snappy solutions. When we slow down, we are more likely to listen...."

—LES AND LESLIE PARROTT[1]

CHAPTER 9

COMMUNICATION: A KEY TO NAVIGATING MARITAL DIFFERENCES

*Do not let any unwholesome talk come out of your
mouths, but only what is helpful for building others up
according to their needs, that it may benefit those who
listen.*

—EPHESIANS 4:29

WITHOUT QUESTION, IT is vitally important to learn how to communicate effectively in marriage. This enables you and your spouse to work through and counter the many potential negative influences that often crop up in your relationship.

When couples come into my office, they often report that the main problem in their marriage is a lack of communication. Interestingly, what I often find is that a lack of communication is just the tip of the iceberg. There is so much more at work below the surface. There is a lack of emotional connection, a lack of feeling valued and secure, and major challenges navigating their personality differences. Add to all this, they lack communication skills, which is the "rudder" that drives the communication ship.

Essentially, there are four basic elements to effective communication. They are *imparting information, listening, understanding, and resolving issues.* Grasping and implementing each of these fundamental parts is important to communicating effectively. In this chapter, we will focus on these basic elements, along with the potential pitfalls that can come with them.

Imparting Information

The first element in communication is *imparting information*—getting a message across to someone. Mankind originally invented language so that we might have the ability to communicate with one another. And if we are going to engage in a conversation, there must be information involved.

In the process of imparting information, there are two potential pitfalls you need to be aware of.

The four basic elements to effective communication are: imparting information, listening, understanding, and resolving issues.

PITFALL 1
NOT ENOUGH / TOO MUCH INFORMATION

One potential problem with imparting information is not giving enough information to the receiver. This is often the case with those on the more assertive end of the spectrum. They tend to have the mindset of "just give me the facts" and often leave out important details in their communication. Having too little information often makes it challenging to really grasp what a person is trying to say. This creates the perfect conditions for misunderstandings and false assumptions to creep in.

Say I draw a dot on a whiteboard and ask you to tell me what it is a picture of. You would likely respond, "I don't know what the picture is. It's just a dot." To this, I might respond, "What do you mean you do not know what it is a picture of? It's as clear as day to me!" The problem is that I have not given you enough dots for you to make sense of my picture. The more dots I put on the board, the clearer the picture will become.

It is the same with communication. The more information you and your spouse have regarding an issue, the more you are able to make sense of what each of you is trying to communicate. The less information you have, the greater the chance you will misinterpret and/or misunderstand what the other is trying to say. Wherever these "informational holes" are found, a communication breakdown is bound to take place.

The solution is for both of you to give enough information (facts and context) so that you each have a clear grasp of what is being communicated. I encourage you to approach communication with your spouse and others by asking yourself, *What do I need to say to ensure my message isn't misunderstood?*

A second problem in imparting information is saying too much at once. Do you or your spouse tend to go on and on in conversations and rarely come up for air? Releasing a flood of information makes it difficult for the hearer to follow or make sense of what is being said. "I just can't seem to concentrate," the person on the receiving end will often tell me. "It's like trying to drink from a fire hydrant. I lose track of the topic of discussion and forget the points that I want to make." In great frustration, the person on the receiving end will typically interrupt their spouse to get a word in edgewise, which only serves to create more tension and conflict in the relationship.

If this is something you and your spouse are experiencing, I encourage you to train yourselves to take turns speaking for one to two minutes at a time. This will effectively stop the flow of communication long enough to allow the other person to ask questions of clarification and respond. Communicating in bite-size portions will allow for more productive and fruitful conversation. Our brains are wired to take in only so much information at a time. Speaking in smaller amounts will actually serve to cover more ground and get more topics adequately addressed in a shorter period.

The more information you and your spouse have regarding an issue, the more you are able to make sense of what the other is trying to communicate.

PITFALL 2
IMPARTING INFORMATION POORLY

Another potential problem in imparting information is the way we deliver it. People who communicate poorly can come across as very short, abrasive, and/or intimidating. Their communication is like a "porcupine in a balloon factory"—sharp, prickly, and explosive. Attempting to have a discussion with them is like having an argument with a prosecuting attorney. They come at you full force and somehow, in the end, they are going to come out on top.

If this is your manner of communicating, you need to realize the impact you are having—especially on your spouse. As the receiver, it often feels to them like you are more interested in winning an argument than actually resolving it. Consequently, they don't feel safe engaging in conversations with you. They feel as if they will simply get minimized or run over. Or, at the very least, they will tune you out because they do not like the way they are being addressed.

In Ephesians 4:15, God instructs us through the apostle Paul that we are to *speak the truth in love* to one another. If I were to boil effective communication down to five words it would be just that: "Speak the truth in love!"

Speaking the truth has to do with being open and honest with one another. We will rarely resolve any issue without being truthful. Reality must be faced and placed on the table. If you have a tendency to be an "avoider" in life like I was years ago, you need to learn how to be more open and honest with your thoughts and feelings. This will happen as you begin to face and defeat any fear of failure and rejection issues you may have, or whatever else drives you to be an avoider.

Speaking *in love* has to do with *how* we communicate the truth. This includes not only our choice of words, but also our non-verbal communication cues like our tone of voice, our attitude, and our body language. If you are the more assertive one in your marriage, it is important that you watch how you are communicating truth to your spouse. I often have the spouse on the receiving end of the conversation say, "It's not what they say that bothers me, but *how* they say it!" Be careful to guard against the potential of coming across as demanding, harsh, and critical.

People often view conflict as negative when, in fact, it is neutral. While it is true that conflict arises from a difference of opinion, we are the ones who make it a pleasant or unpleasant experience by the way that we handle our disagreements. I believe that when we have disagreements, we can choose to handle them in a calm and civil manner that mutually respects, seeks understanding, and works towards productive resolutions.

Ephesians 4:29 says, "Do not let any unwholesome talk come out of your mouths, but only what is helpful for building others up according to their needs, that it may benefit those who listen." Wow! What an incredible guide for communication. If you and your spouse will follow these words of wisdom, speaking in ways that are helpful and with the goal of building each other up, resolving conflict will be much more inviting and productive. We will shed more light on this subject in Chapter 10 when we address the topic of *negotiation*.

Effective communication can be boiled down to five simple words: "Speak the truth in love!"

Listening

The second element in effective communication is *actively listening* to what is being said. If we do not carefully listen, we will not know how to respond or what action to take.

Has this happened to you? Has your spouse been talking to you, and you were caught *not* listening? After they were finished speaking, they asked a question, and you just stared at them. In desperation, you tried to figure out what they said and come up with an intelligent response, but because you weren't listening, you had no idea of what they were talking about.

Don't feel bad. I think we have all been caught not listening. To help you become a better listener, here are a couple of potential pitfalls you need to be aware of.

PITFALL 1
FAILING TO PAY ATTENTION

One breakdown in listening is the *failure to pay attention* when someone is speaking. This happens when we let our mind wander when someone is trying to get a point across. Or, we may be focusing on what *we want to say* in return instead of what is being said to us. We think we already know what our spouse (or someone else) is communicating, so we begin formulating our response without really listening to their message.

Failing to engage in effective listening does not make for fruitful and productive conversation. For one thing, we often miss some key information that is being conveyed that will enlighten us about a situation. For another, it may communicate to the other party that we think we are above them, or that we simply do not care.

I remember a number of occasions when I was talking to someone in a crowd, and I could tell their eyes were wandering all over the place. It was evident that they were not really listening to what I had to say or engaging with me. In today's world, this distraction level is an even greater problem as people are constantly interacting on their mobile phones or electronic gadgets while they are supposed to be engaged in conversation.

Whatever the reason for failing to pay attention, not actively listening to someone we are talking with will ultimately send them the message that we really don't care. It also communicates that what we care about is more important than them. We must make it our aim to give others our undivided attention when they are speaking to us.

Be a good listener. Make it your aim to give others your undivided attention when they are speaking.

PITFALL 2
INTERRUPTING

Another enemy of effective listening is *interrupting*. When we keep interrupting someone when they are speaking to us, we are indirectly sending them a message: "What *you* have to say is not important. What *I* have to say is much more important." Ultimately, interrupting others is rude and disrespectful.

I remember one couple I worked with several years ago that were constantly interrupting one another during our counseling sessions. Neither got more than two or three words out before the other cut them off. It was like watching a ping pong match as my head perpetually turned from one to the other. Their conversation quickly escalated to the point where neither party was even hearing what the other was saying. I finally put my hand up and said, "Time out. I cannot even follow what is going on here, and it is becoming very unproductive. You both need to do something different."

I have heard some people say that they interrupt because they don't want to forget some important information that they want to get across at a key moment. If this is the case for you, I encourage you to make a mental note or keep a piece of paper handy to write down your thoughts so that you can share them when it is your turn to speak.

If you and your spouse are having trouble interrupting each other, I encourage you to try this helpful exercise. Take a small object like a pen or pencil, and the one who is talking is to hold it in their hand. I suggest that the one who has the object take one to two minutes to speak before handing it to the other person. Getting too longwinded may overwhelm the other person's ability to patiently wait to speak.

Remember, whoever holds the object gets to talk, and the other person's job is to listen. When the person talking has used all of their time, they are to hand the object to the other person. The first job of the person who receives the object is to reflect back on what they heard the other say to make certain they understood them correctly. If this is you, you would look at your spouse and say something like, "So, what I'm hearing you say is…" and then repeat what you heard them say. Then you would have the opportunity to talk, and your spouse who passed the object listens.

The goal of this exercise is to promote more purposeful listening, ensure better understanding, and effectively cut out the inattention and interruptions. This also creates disciplined communication with respect and promotes overall peace in your marriage.

Communicating in bite-size portions of 1-2 minutes will allow for more productive and fruitful conversations.

UNDERSTANDING

Unquestionably, the most important element of communication is in *understanding*. Interestingly, understanding is typically the most neglected factor in communication between individuals. Couples typically report to me that in their communication pattern there is some imparting information, less active listening, and very little understanding going on between them. It is imperative that we understand both the *message* and the *motive* of what is being communicated.

The **message** is *what* you are communicating. It is the actual information that you are attempting to get across. It is imperative that you and your spouse are both hearing and operating with the same set of facts.

The **motive** is *why* you are communicating the message. It is the heart or purpose of your message. To effectively communicate, we must also understand the motive or intent of the message. That being said, here are two potential pitfalls to you need to be aware of regarding understanding.

PITFALL 1
MISINTERPRETATION OR MISUNDERSTANDING

One potential pitfall of understanding someone is to *misinterpret* what they said. To misinterpret a message means that we don't have the right set of facts. In essence, we create our own private meaning and/or motive of the communicator's real intent. Typically, when we misinterpret a situation, we also misunderstand it.

Many times when I am working through issues with couples, one will say to the other, "Oh, I didn't know that was what you meant when you said that to me. I thought what you were saying was…" and they share something quite different than what was intended. Sadly, the one who misinterpreted the facts had already been extremely upset over something that was never meant or intended. They could have saved everyone involved a lot of grief had they taken the time to make certain they had a proper understanding of the message.

To help limit misinterpretation and improve understanding between you and your spouse, I suggest using one or more of these communication tools to make sure you have the proper meaning and motive of their message. The first tool is *clarification*. To clarify is to tell your spouse in your own words what you think they said. This helps to make certain you understand what they are actually saying.

Another way to minimize misinterpretation is by *summarizing* what your spouse said. Like clarification, summarizing gives them the opportunity to clear up any misunderstandings you may have concerning their message and intent. A third tool to help reduce misinterpretation is to *ask questions* to gather information and make certain you are on the right track with what they are communicating. Clarification, summarizing, and asking questions are three tools that will go a long way to promote understanding and preserving the peace in your marriage.

Three tools to help improve understanding are clarification, summarizing, and asking questions.

PITFALL 2
MAKING ASSUMPTIONS

Probably the biggest killer of communication and relationships in general is *making assumptions*. To make an assumption means that we concoct a private guess as to what another person's message and motive are. Husbands and wives do this frequently. Rather than directly speaking to each other to openly gather information and the facts regarding a situation, we conjure up our own interpretation of their motive. Unfortunately, when we make assumptions we usually believe the worst-case scenario. As a result, we become upset and offended over what typically turns out to be untrue.

Several years ago, I served as a mediator between two families in a small town. They had been embroiled in conflict for over two years. It was so severe that several of the family members had not even spoken to one another the entire time. Imagine this dynamic in a small town in which most people knew each other by name. Once we were finally able to get two of the opposing family members together and they started telling their stories, they realized that the whole two-year feud was based on a misunderstanding of an event. Openly, they both wept as they pondered all the hurt, anger, resentment, bitterness, and years of silence they endured over something that wasn't even true.

Indeed, one of the worst things you and I can do in relationships is to assume motives. This hazardous practice often flows from a lack of being open and honest with others. When we are afraid of being truthful with people, we tend to hide our true thoughts and feelings and then fail to ask for truth from others. Another way we assume people's motives is by failing to get the true facts of a situation. We abruptly make our own private assessment regarding a situation, and before long we are off and running with our often faulty interpretation.

When we don't have the truth, we are left to make assumptions regarding situations. Being the fallen creatures that we are, we usually take things personally and assume the worst. Whatever you do, make certain you have the correct information and an accurate understanding of the situation before you judge someone or make a comment. Get the message and the motive straight! You will save yourself and others much heartache.

RESOLVING ISSUES

Resolving issues is the fourth basic element of effective communication. It means we are able to adequately resolve a disagreement. Resolution may come in the form of coming to a common understanding or an agreement regarding an issue. It may also happen when we are able to effectively negotiate a solution and/or reach a compromise (more on this in Chapter 10). Finally, resolving issues may simply mean that we agree to disagree on something.

Unlike imparting information, listening, and understanding, I have no pitfalls to offer for resolving issues. In my opinion, when people fail to do the first three effectively, there is often little resolution. However, when we take time to carefully impart and receive information, listen well, and make certain we have a proper understanding, we are able to resolve issues effectively.

When we take time to carefully impart and receive information, listen well, and have a proper understanding, we are able to effectively resolve issues.

An Illustration in Marriage

Imagine this: a wife comes home from the grocery store, and her husband asks her a simple question. "Did you buy cookies at the grocery store?"

Almost instantly, she begins to get visibly agitated and upset and finally blurts out, "Why? Do you think I'm overweight and shouldn't be eating sweets? That's what you think, isn't it? You think I should be on a diet, and you're angry with me for buying cookies. I can never make you happy!"

In bewilderment, the husband stares and cautiously replies, "No, my sweet tooth is rearing its ugly head, and I was actually hoping you brought cookies home."

Let's examine what's happening in this situation.

First, the husband didn't give enough information to his wife for her to make sense of what he was communicating. While he asked a simple question, he left it open to several interpretations. Had he given more information and said something like, "Hey honey, did you buy cookies at the grocery store? My sweet tooth is rearing its ugly head, and I'm dying for a cookie," he would have diffused the whole situation and saved himself a good tongue lashing. So, the husband could have been clearer in his message to his wife to ensure that she did not misinterpret him.

The wife, on the other hand, wrongly assumed her husband's motive. She made an assumption that he thought she was overweight and shouldn't be buying or eating sweets. She significantly misinterpreted both his message and his motive. Had she asked some questions of clarification, she would not have gotten all upset over what was not true. She could have responded with something like, "Can you help me understand why you're asking me if I bought cookies? What is the purpose of your question?" Asking simple questions like these would have given her husband a chance to respond with more information, and the truth would have come out.

This illustration is a common example of the breakdown in communication. The key to overcoming situations like these is to adequately and thoroughly move through each step of the communication process.

One: Give enough information and allow your spouse to ask clarifying questions. This ensures that you both have the correct and intended message.

Two: Listen carefully to what is being said. This means respecting one another enough to engage and hear one another out.

Three: Make sure you both understand the message and motive of what is being communicated. This ensures you are both operating out of the same set of facts.

By repeating these three steps throughout a conversation, you and your spouse will likely resolve issues and avoid unnecessary arguments.

As we close this chapter, I want to give you what I call *Dave's "Cliff Notes" on Communication*. These six principles cut to the heart of the typical downfalls of communication. By simply following these principles, you will greatly improve your communication with your spouse and others.

Dave's Cliff Notes on Communication

1. Start your conversation by affirming the other person. Say something positive. This will automatically take them off of the defensive and set a right, healthy tone.

2. State your motive clearly upfront. Don't give them room to wrongly assume your motives or intensions.

3. Make certain that you are giving enough information (providing the full context) for the receiver to accurately understand what you are communicating.

4. If you don't understand something they have said, ask questions to clarify or gather more information. Don't assume!

5. Watch for *how* you are communicating. Speak the truth in a loving and respectful way that encourages dialogue rather than shutting the other person down.

6. Head assumptions off at the pass by starting with something like, "Now don't hear what I am not saying."

CHAPTER SUMMARY 9

There are four basic elements to effective communication: *imparting information, listening, understanding,* and *resolving issues.* We need to give our spouse enough information (the "context") and allow them to ask clarifying questions to ensure we both have the correct message (the "facts"). We must listen attentively and respectfully when they are speaking. And we must seek to accurately understand what has been said. When we take time to carefully impart and receive information, listen well, and make certain we have a proper understanding, we are able to effectively resolve issues.

(1) Les and Leslie Parrott, *Like a Kiss on the Lips* (Grand Rapids, MI: Zondervan Publishing House, 1997, p. 60).

Making It Yours ────────────────────────────

1. Of the four basic elements of communication—*imparting information, listening, understanding,* and *resolving issues*—which would you say is the greatest challenge in your marriage? Why do you believe this to be the case? How is this chapter helping you see things differently?

   Our greatest communication challenge in our marriage is...

   _____

   This seems to be the case because...

   _____

   _____

   This chapter on communication is helping me see things differently in the following ways:

   _____

   _____

   _____

2. What practical adjustments do you feel God is prompting you to make regarding your communication with your spouse? How can you come up higher in these areas?

   The Four Basic Elements: Imparting Information, Listening, Understanding, Resolving Issues

   _____

   _____

   _____

   Word Choice and Non-Verbal Cues (Tone of Voice, Attitude, and Body Language)

   _____

   _____

   _____

163

3. God has much to say in His Word about the way we talk to one another. Carefully read these passages and jot down what He is speaking and revealing to you in each regarding your communication.

Ephesians 4:15, 29-32

_____

_____

Colossians 4:6

_____

_____

Proverbs 10:19; 17:27-28

_____

_____

_____

James 1:26; Proverbs 13:3; 21:23; Psalm 141:3-4

_____

_____

_____

For further study, carefully read Proverbs 10 and James 3:2-10.

Once you and your spouse have each answered the questions individually, sit together and ask him or her to go through the questions with you. Share your answers with each other. How are your answers similar? Where are they different?

"I challenge you to see any disagreements with your spouse as a doorway to intimacy. Let conflicts be that doorway into a better understanding of how you both feel and what you each need."

—GARY SMALLEY[1]

CHAPTER 10

NEGOTIATION: THE PATHWAY TO PARTNERSHIP AND GREATER INTIMACY

"Do nothing out of selfish ambition or vain conceit, but in humility consider others better than yourselves. Each of you should look not only to your own interests, but also to the interests of others."

—PHILIPPIANS 2:3-4

ALONG WITH THE tool of communication that I laid out in the last chapter, *negotiation* is another effective instrument to maintain a healthy marriage. It is especially useful when we have decisions to make or we need to come to an agreement concerning a matter.

Some issues are small, like deciding where you and your spouse will go out to eat, where you will go on vacation, or what color to paint a particular room. Other issues are more significant, such as how you will handle your finances, how you will discipline your kids, or if you should move to a new city.

The more you avoid issues, or one of you dominates the other by continually making decisions apart from the other, the less intimacy and togetherness you will share in your marriage. On the contrary, the more you and your spouse come together to negotiate and resolve issues, the more you will build partnership and intimacy in your relationship.

I would say that for almost every issue you and your spouse face, if you will humble yourselves and truly work at it, you can come to some kind of an agreement or compromise. There are few issues in which we become so completely polarized that we simply cannot agree on how to handle them. It is usually our personalities, our individual perspectives, and our personal desires that get in the way of coming together on decisions.

Although there are times when we may need to "agree to disagree," I find this to be the *exception* more than the rule. What we definitely don't want to do is go in to a situation with the mentality that there is going to be a *winner* and a *loser*. This competitive perspective means that someone is going to get the short end of the stick—a raw deal. An approach of this nature creates a combative atmosphere right from the start and does not set the stage for fruitful negotiation. Therefore, it is most important to take time to actively hear one another out and get to the roots of the issue at hand. Go into the negotiation process with the mentality of looking for a win/win outcome.

The more you and your spouse come together to negotiate and work to resolve issues, the more you will build partnership and intimacy in your relationship.

167

We Are Constantly Faced with *Issues*

Every day you and I have to deal with issues, especially in our marriage. What greater tool to resolve relational conflict than healthy negotiation? It is important to note that with every negotiation, there are three factors involved: an *issue*, a *position*, and an *interest*.

Basically, an *issue* comes in the form of a question; it is the matter that needs to be addressed. The issue is always the *same* for both parties. When one arises, a decision must be made to resolve it. Some examples of issues that may develop between you and your spouse include:

- Where do we want to go to eat tonight?
- Where should we go on vacation this year?
- Should we buy a new car or a used car?
- How should we handle our finances?
- How should we discipline our children?

With Each Issue, We Take a *Position*

A *position* is each person's answer to the question at hand. *Your* position is what you think should be done regarding the issue. Your spouse has a position too. This is where the disagreement and potential conflict occur—the place where differing positions concerning an issue arise. Here are some potential positions that might arise regarding the above issues:

Restaurant - I would like to go out for Chinese.
Vacation - I would like to go to the beach this spring.
Car - I think we should buy a used car.

Money - I think we should save 20 percent of our income each month.

Children - I think that children should never be spanked.

When both parties are in agreement, issues are simple to resolve. It would be great if we agreed on everything. If we did, we would never get into arguments. However, that is unrealistic. The truth is we have different personalities, tastes, backgrounds, and experiences. Therefore, we often have differing opinions or desires, which create ample opportunities for healthy negotiation. The higher the stakes in a situation, the more challenging it is to negotiate.

With every negotiation, there are three factors involved:
an issue, a position, and an interest.

Our Position is Based on Personal *Interest*

An *interest* is the "why" behind the position we hold. It is the heart motive for why you and I think or feel the way we do concerning an issue. Our interest is the "driver" of our position. Again, in light of the original issues and possible positions presented, here are some potential interests:

Restaurant – I was looking forward to the variety of food that they have.

Vacation – I would like to simply relax and soak up the sun.

Car – We will save money if we buy used. New cars lose value the second you drive them off the lot, and the property taxes are higher.

Money – I really want to be saving for our future. I would like to try to retire early.

Children – There are more effective ways to discipline children, and I feel that spanking is damaging and inappropriate to a child.

SEEK TO UNDERSTAND ONE ANOTHER

In order to successfully negotiate an issue, it is vital to take the time to completely understand your spouse's *personal interest*. Remember, a person's interest is the ultimate driver of their position, so we need to take the time to understand why their position is so important to them. The more you thoroughly understand each other's interests the better you will be able to come up with a productive compromise.

As I work with couples they typically admit that their attempts at negotiation rarely ever get to or focus on the interest level. For instance, one scenario I have seen repeatedly is when one or both parties begin to assert their position and then quickly butt heads over why their way is the better way to go. Sadly, neither spouse bothers to listen to the other regarding each other's interest. As a result, they both get upset, hurt, and offended because they feel ignored and misunderstood.

Another common scenario I've seen is when one person abruptly and definitively asserts their position so strongly that the other shuts down. The one whose interest is squelched gives in quickly and doesn't even bother to mention, much less defend, their position. Unfortunately, this person eventually becomes resentful at "never having a say" in matters. A position driven approach to negotiation rarely works. This is why it is so important to spend the bulk of your time at the interest level.

To successfully negotiate an issue, it is important to take time to learn your spouse's interest.

SHARE PERSONAL INSIGHTS

After spending quality time hearing each other out, you should spend equal time hearing each other's *personal insights* regarding the issue. Personal insights are everything that you know regarding a situation. For instance, you may want to go to a certain place for vacation and I happen to know that you are planning on going during the rain season. As a result, we may end up spending our whole vacation indoors. Personal insights help both parties have as much information as possible before making a final informed decision.

ADDRESS KEY CONCERNS

Another important factor is to address any *key concerns* each of you have about the issue. Key concerns are cautions or apprehensions I may have regarding the decision we are making. If I want to buy a certain used car your key concern may be that we don't know where the car has come from or its history. We may be buying a lemon or someone else's problems. Addressing key concerns will assure more confidence by both parties in moving forward with a decision and build unity in the process.

In the end, the more information you have concerning one another's personal insights and concerns, the more informed you will be. Consequently, the more open and flexible you will be to adapt and adjust to your spouse's position (or at least willing to reach a compromise).

TAKE TIME TO BRAINSTORM

The next phase of negotiation is to *brainstorm ideas* on how to adequately and commonly address the issue. At this stage, it doesn't matter how crazy your ideas might sound. The important thing is to get as many ideas out on the table as possible. You may be surprised at how many "strange" ideas turn out to be good ideas after all. Once you have exhausted all your possibilities, weigh each potential solution for its effectiveness and feasibility.

WORK TOGETHER TO FORM A SOLUTION

Finally comes decision time! After you and your spouse have discussed all your interests, insights, concerns, and ideas, make a quality decision as a team. As you carefully walk through the negotiation process, you will typically be able to come up with some sort of solution or compromise. At the same time, you will both feel validated, respected, and understood. This will build partnership, unity, and intimacy in your marriage which is ultimately more important than the issue itself.

MEET BEN AND JULIE

AN EXAMPLE OF HOW NEGOTIATION TAKES PLACE

THE WRONG WAY

Ben and Julie are excited about going out for dinner. They have been looking forward to this all week. The sitter is in place, and all they need to do is select a restaurant.

"Where would you like to go tonight, Julie?" Ben asks.

"I'd love Chinese," she replies. "The buffet has so many enjoyable dishes!"

"Aw, not Chinese," Ben moans. "I'll go anywhere but there. How about Italian?"

Vividly upset, Julie combatively snaps, "We always go where *you* want to go. Why can't we go where *I* want to go for a change?"

"I'm not going out for Chinese!" Ben rants.

"Fine!" shouts Julie. "If you want Italian, you can go by yourself! I'm going out for Chinese!"

In a whirlwind, both Julie and Ben fly out the door, get into separate cars and drive away.

---

*After spending time hearing each other out, spend
equal time hearing each other's personal insights and
key concerns regarding the issue.*

THE RIGHT WAY

Let's hit rewind and replay this scenario, employing the process of healthy negotiation. Again, Ben and Julie are going out to dinner and just need to select a place in which to dine.

"Where would you like to go tonight, Julie?" Ben asks. [This is the **issue**.]

"I'd love Chinese," she replies. "The buffet has so many enjoyable dishes!" [This is *Julie's* **position**.]

"Aw, not Chinese," Ben moans. "I'll go anywhere but there. How about Italian?" [This is *Ben's* **position**.]

"Can you help me understand why you don't want to go out for Chinese?" Julie asks calmly. [She is seeking to understand Ben's **interest**.]

Ben replies, "I had Chinese for lunch the other day, got sick to my stomach, and lost it all about an hour later in the bathroom. I don't think that I can handle Chinese today." [This is Ben's **key concern**.]

"Oh, I understand. So sorry you got sick, Ben. Let's pick another type of food. I'm not really in the mood for Italian myself. How about Mexican?" [Julie has now begun to **brainstorm** solutions.]

"That sounds perfect!" Ben says with a smile. [He and Julie have reached a **compromise**.]

Julie grabs her purse and Ben his jacket. He opens the door, and the two climb into the car and head toward the restaurant—together and in a peaceful state. What a difference!

God's Word says, "Congenial conversation—what a pleasure! The right word at the right time—beautiful!" (Proverbs 15:23 MSG). Indeed, "the right word at the right time is like a custom-made piece of jewelry" (Proverbs 25:11 MSG).

Two Potential Dynamics to Be Aware of

There are a couple of things you need to be aware of as you begin to put negotiation into practice, and they have to deal with your personalities.

First of all, if you are the one on the more *assertive* end of the spectrum, you may come across to your spouse as more position-driven and less concerned about their interest or them as a person. Coming into the negotiation, you will already know what you want or think should happen regarding the issue. As a result, your focus will tend to be more on lobbying for your position than truly understanding their position and interest and negotiating.

So be careful not to quickly dismiss or shoot down your spouse's position. Instead, *actively listen* to his or her interest. Having a more passive personality, he or she will be put in the place of having to defend their position or trying to prove it is the better way to go. If you don't make the needed adjustments, this winner/loser, courtroom-approach negotiation will not promote the unity and peace you are both looking for.

A winner/loser, courtroom-approach negotiation will not promote the unity and peace you and your spouse are looking for.

A second thing to keep in mind is for those who are on the more *passive* end of the spectrum. If this is you, you will have a tendency to not even bring issues up for discussion. You either don't see the situation as an issue or you don't want to argue. Thus, you keep things to yourself.

If you are the more passive one, you will also need to guard against surrendering your interest too quickly. Instead of just giving in to your spouse's position for the sake of "peace and harmony," make a decision to kindly, yet firmly, stand and exert your position. By doing so, you will greatly diminish the danger of becoming resentful of your spouse, which often happens when this dynamic is at play. At the same time, you will help him or her to not develop a lack of respect for you and not give you a voice because you are not as assertive.

Through it all, I encourage you to resist the temptation of allowing the negotiation process to become position-driven. If you or your spouse feels as though you are in a courtroom defending or pushing your position, you have crossed the line into position-driven negotiation. This approach breaks down marital unity and undermines your sense of partnership. Interest-driven negotiation, on the other hand, builds mutual respect, fosters oneness, and will further intimacy in your marriage.

Remember, the key to effective negotiation is to quickly get to the interest level and spend the bulk of your time there. The more time you take to understand one another and the motives of your hearts, the more likely it is that you will come to a healthy compromise. Also, remember that your marriage relationship is ultimately more important than the issue at hand.

Chapter Summary 10

Negotiation is a useful tool to help couples make good decisions and come to an agreement on any matter we face. With every negotiation, there are three factors: an *issue*, a *position*, and an *interest*. While the issue is the matter that needs to be addressed, the position is each person's answer to solving the issue. And the interest is the "why" behind our position. The bulk of your time in negotiation should be spent at the interest level, understanding each other's heart and motive behind your positions. The more you and your spouse come together to negotiate and resolve issues, the more you will build partnership and intimacy in your relationship.

(1) Gary Smalley, *Making Love Last Forever* (Dallas, TX: Word Publishing, 1996, p. 230).

Author's Note: *Some of the information in this chapter was adapted from the training I received through Peacemaker Ministries. For more information, visit www.peacemaker.net.*

Making It Yours ────────────────────────────────

1. We all face challenging issues in marriage, but with God's help we can learn to negotiate and work with our spouse instead of working against them. Stop and think: What are *the top three recurring issues* you seem to face repeatedly? Do you see any common threads between them? If so, what are they? **Our Top Three Recurring Issues Are:**

   _____

   _____

   _____

2. To help you and your spouse learn and/or improve the process of negotiating, take the three recurring issues you wrote down in Question 1 and walk through the steps, using the negotiation worksheet I have created. It is based on God's Words to us in Philippians 2:1-4. Carefully read through the passage and then work through each issue you are facing, identifying and writing down the essential elements.

   If you have any encouragement from being united with Christ, if any comfort from his love, if any fellowship with the Spirit, if any tenderness and compassion, then make my joy complete by being like-minded, having the same love, being one in spirit and purpose. Do nothing out of selfish ambition or vain conceit, but in humility consider others better than yourselves. Each of you should look not only to your own interests, but also to the interests of the others.

   —PHILIPPIANS 2:1-4

NEGOTIATION WORKSHEET
Philippians 2:1-4

YOUR SPOUSE   YOU

_____ ISSUE _____

_____ POSITION _____

_____ INTEREST _____

_____PERSONAL INSIGHTS_____

_____ KEY CONCERNS _____

_____ BRAINSTORM SOLUTIONS _____

_____ A GOOD COMPROMISE _____

3. Look back at the top three recurring conflicts you and your spouse are experiencing. Put yourself in his/her shoes. Attempt to look at the situations from their perspective (their upbringing, experiences, and being married to you). How do you see these issues affecting them personally? How do the situations appear different through their eyes? How is this exercise helping you to adapt and be willing to work towards a compromise?

    The ways I see these challenging situations affecting my spouse are...

    _____

    _____

    _____

    I am able to see these situations differently through their eyes in the following ways:

179

_____

_____

_____

Seeking to understand these situations from my spouse's perspective encourages me to...

_____

_____

_____

"In truth, forgiveness is a *choice*, a spiritual discipline, rather than a feeling. If you wait for the supposed emotional motivation, you will quite probably spend much of your life in a self-made prison. Learn to act out your forgiveness, and you will discover a life of joy and freedom."

—**RICHARD EXLEY**[1]

CHAPTER 11

RECONCILIATION: THE MEANS
OF MAINTAINING PEACE

*Let us therefore make every effort to do what leads to
peace and to mutual edification.*

—ROMANS 14:19

WHAT HAPPENS ONCE you and your spouse have hurt and offended
one another? How do you regain and maintain peace and harmony in the midst of your differences, wounds, and wrongdoings?
How can you keep resentment and bitterness from creeping into
your marriage? This is accomplished through the continuing
process of *reconciliation.*

As I mentioned in Chapter 7, maintaining peace and harmony in marriage is vital to the emotional connection (or disconnection) that we feel toward one another. Avoiding or mishandling
conflict will only serve to widen the wedge of relational distance
between you and your spouse.

In this chapter, we will examine a proven recipe for reconciliation. It is a four-step process that begins with *getting our
hearts out on the table* and continues as we work through *repentance, forgiveness,* and *change.* The key to experiencing successful

reconciliation is to be continually engaged in the process, removing any barriers that keep you and your spouse from coming together and preserving peace and harmony in your relationship.

STEP 1

GET YOUR HEARTS OUT ON THE TABLE

The first step in the reconciliation process is to *get our hearts out on the table*. Our heart is the very core of who we are and the greatest driving force in our life. In Proverbs 4:23 we read, "Above all else, guard your heart, for it is the wellspring of life." And in Luke 6:45, Jesus declares that we speak out of the overflow, or abundance, of what is in our heart. What do these verses reveal? In order for genuine reconciliation to take place, it is imperative that we discover and deal with what is in our heart. In other words, we need to openly share our true thoughts and feelings with our spouse, not keep them locked up inside. As we both share what is going on in our worlds regarding how we have been hurt and offended, we can guard our hearts from the growth of resentment and bitterness.

Reconciliation is a four-step process that includes repentance, forgiveness, change, and getting our hearts out on the table.

Picture a husband and wife sitting in an elegant restaurant surrounded by a group of their closest friends. His name is Pete and her name is Samantha. The conversation is flowing, and laughter rhythmically fills the air. Suddenly, Pete makes a funny but cutting remark about his wife in front of their friends. They all laugh but Samantha feels embarrassed, humiliated, and betrayed by her husband.

Samantha has three choices as to how she will handle the offense. One choice is to go ballistic on Pete and ream him out for his behavior after they leave the restaurant. This approach will most likely shut her husband down or turn into a heated argument, which will lessen the chance for reconciliation. A second option is for Samantha to hide her true feelings and say nothing to Pete. With this approach, she will most likely become resentful over time and emotionally detached from her husband. In addition, she could make his life miserable through her words and actions, but not tell him why she is upset (a classic passive-aggressive response).

A third choice for Samantha is to go to Pete and share her heart concerning the hurt and betrayal she feels as a result of his actions. This option has the best chance for genuine reconciliation. It honors God and positions them to restore and experience peace and harmony in their marriage again.

STEP 2

REPENT

The second step in the reconciliation process is to *repent*. Genuine repentance includes *remorse* or *sorrow* for the damage we have caused to someone else. In Second Corinthians 7:10 we read, "Godly sorrow brings repentance that leads to salvation and leaves no regret, but worldly sorrow brings death."

There is a vast difference between godly sorrow and worldly sorrow. Godly sorrow is being remorseful over the wrongdoing that we have committed before God and others. It is a genuine regret that we have offended God and hurt the people we love through our actions and/or words. This is the kind of repentance we see from King David in Psalm 51 as he pours his heart out to God concerning his sin. Worldly sorrow, on the other hand, is feeling sorry for ourselves that we got caught. This is the kind of sorrow we often view on the evening news when people are given sentences for a crime they have committed. Their tears are often not because they have hurt and offended others, but because of the consequences they will have to face for their crime.

Genuine repentance also includes *accepting responsibility* for our actions. This may come in the form of going to others and admitting that we have done something wrong. It may also involve making some sort of restitution financially, or by giving our time to compensate for our actions. Accepting responsibility means we face and receive the consequences of our actions. When I work with couples in which one has been involved in an affair, one of the consequences of the offending party is to regularly let their spouse know where they are and what they are doing. This heightened level of accountability is the way they will ultimately rebuild trust in their spouse.

Finally, repentance that is sincere involves *genuine confession*. A genuine confession consists of at least these three important elements: First, *we honestly admit what we have done* to the offended person(s). Next, *we acknowledge the damage and the hurt we have caused* them. And third, *we work to transform our behavior into something better.* When we honestly and sincerely walk out these three aspects, walls come down and hearts begin to mend. In my opinion and experience the key to adequate repentance is in specifically admitting what we have done and acknowledging the hurt we have caused.

Genuine repentance includes confessing what we have done, accepting responsibility for our actions, and sincerely expressing sorrow for the hurt we have caused.

Going back to our earlier example, suppose Samantha chooses to go to her husband Pete and get her heart out on the table. Saddened, she informs him through tears how she felt hurt and humiliated by his remarks. More importantly, she explains how she felt betrayed by him, the one person present who was supposed to be loyal and protect her from harm. With this done, the ball is now in Pete's court. It is up to him as to how he responds.

Pete has at least three options. One option is to ignore her comments and walk away, hoping the situation will simply disappear and work itself out. A second option is to make light of the situation and turn it back on his wife. "Aw come on, Samantha," he might say. "You're making a mountain out of a mole hill. It wasn't really that big of a deal. You're just too sensitive about these things. I was only having fun." This choice will simply inflict further hurt and cause relational damage and alienation.

A third option Pete has is to face the issue head-on and accept responsibility for his actions. This is repentance—the correct, godly option that will lead to reconciliation, healing, and peace. With this option, he would respond by saying something like, "You're right. I did put you down and make fun of you in front of our friends. I was wrong to do that. I am the one who is supposed to protect you from harm, not harm you. I can see how you would feel hurt and betrayed by what I said. If you want, I'll go back to our friends and tell them I was wrong for what I did. I will also do my best to never do that again. With God's help, I will make it my aim to affirm you in front of others." This is true repentance. It is taking ownership and acknowledging our wrongdoing. It is genuinely repenting and seeking forgiveness for our offenses. It is the only pathway to experiencing true freedom and inner peace.

STEP 3

FORGIVE

The third step in the reconciliation process is to *forgive*. Typically, when someone genuinely repents of their actions, forgiveness follows. This, however, can be delayed due to the severity of the offense. It is one thing to put your spouse down in public. It is quite another to have a five-year affair whereby you have a child with an adulterous partner. Typically, the more severe the offense, the more time we need to give for healing and forgiveness to take place. Still, it is honoring to God and to everyone's advantage to take the path of reconciliation and over time choose to forgive.

Some of the most miserable, angry, and depressed people I have ever met are those who choose to hold on to their anger and bitterness and refuse to attempt to move toward forgiveness. While I am definitely not minimizing the hurtful and damaging experiences we encounter, I am saying that it is to one's own advantage to eventually move toward forgiveness. Not to do so will often produce worse consequences than the actual offense itself.

---

*It is honoring to God and to everyone's advantage to
take the path of reconciliation and choose to forgive,
regardless of how long it takes.*

So what does it mean to forgive? Good question. Let me begin by sharing what...

FORGIVENESS IS NOT

FORGIVENESS IS *NOT* (PRIMARILY) A FEELING. In order to forgive someone, you don't have to *feel* like you can forgive them. Although feelings are important, it is often through the act of forgiveness itself that feelings follow. It is true that we often need time to process the pain and heal, but if you and I wait until we "feel" like forgiving, we may never get around to it.

FORGIVENESS IS *NOT* LETTING GO OF ALL EMOTIONS. When you chose to forgive someone, it does not mean that you may never feel angry or hurt over the offense again. Forgiveness is not putting on a happy face, stuffing your emotions, and pretending the hurt never happened. It is a choice to acknowledge and then let go of the offense. However, once you and I do choose to forgive, we need to be mindful of how we handle the emotions that surface as we continue to work through the issue.

FORGIVENESS IS *NOT* ACCEPTING THE BEHAVIOR. Choosing to forgive someone does not mean that we are admitting that what they did was okay. Sometimes people are reluctant to forgive because they feel that to do so is sending the message that what the offender did was acceptable. This is not the case. As we have seen, the offender needs to rightly acknowledge the wrongness of their actions.

FORGIVENESS IS *NOT* DOING AWAY WITH CONSEQUENCES. By extending forgiveness, the offender does not get off scot-free. As we have already mentioned, true repentance means accepting the consequences of our actions. If one truly repents, they will willingly do what they need to do to attempt to make up for the offense. Either way, the offender will accept the consequences.

FORGIVENESS IS *NOT* FORGETTING. When you forgive, it does not mean that you have to erase the event from your memory banks and live as if the event never happened. Some painful events may never be completely eliminated from our minds. However, as we rightly move through the reconciliation process and work on the act of forgiveness, over time the event will typically slip into the background of our mind and life.

Forgiveness is not a feeling, it is not forgetting, nor is it accepting wrong behavior or doing away with consequences.

So what is forgiveness?

FORGIVENESS IS

FORGIVENESS IS ULTIMATELY A *COMMAND OF GOD*. First and foremost, we are to extend forgiveness to others because God extends forgiveness to us. Otherwise you and I run the risk of becoming like the unmerciful servant in Matthew 18:21-35. Jesus said this man was forgiven a tremendous debt by the king, but when he went out and found someone who owed him a mere pittance in comparison, the servant would not forgive the debt. The king found out and reinstated the original debt of the servant.

There is a saying that goes, "He who has been forgiven much forgives much." If we are honest with ourselves, we all know deep in our hearts that we continually offend God. Yet He willingly and continually chooses to forgive us. Having a fresh realization of His grace, mercy, and forgiveness in our own lives for our offenses toward Him enables us to forgive others for the offenses they commit towards us. I will say it again. While I don't want to minimize the pain and suffering that we may experience due to the offenses of others, it is to God's glory and for our own healing to eventually come to forgiveness.

FORGIVENESS IS A *CHOICE* WE MAKE. As an act of our free will, we make a pointed decision to choose to forgive others. No one else can do the forgiving for us. We must make that choice on our own.

FORGIVENESS IS *SEEKING A NEW COURSE OF ACTION.* In other words, when we choose to forgive an offense, it's like we post some "warning signs" in our heart and mind and we obey them. These signs include…

No Fishing. Once we choose to forgive, we will not keep bringing up the incident to the forgiven party—even when we get angry. To keep fishing for an offense indicates that we have not truly forgiven the individual for it. We are still harboring something inside.

No Talking. When we choose to forgive incessant talking to our friends and others about how we have been hurt stops. Retelling the details of the event is unproductive. It is one thing to have a trusted friend, confidant, or pastor help us walk toward healing and forgiveness. It is quite another to keep replaying what happened to anyone who will listen. All this kind of talking does is refill our hearts with bitterness and resentment.

No Trespassing. Once we forgive, we don't keep mentally reentering the scene of the offense. It is a no trespassing zone. To the best of our ability, we don't allow ourselves to negatively dwell on the event in an unhealthy manner. Revisiting the offensive incident over and over will only serve to keep it fresh in our hearts and minds.

Forgiveness is a command of God to willingly choose to let go of the offenses of others and seek a new course of action.

To counter negative thoughts, we can replace them with more productive and positive ones. I have found that having key Bible verses to draw from is very helpful. We can also maintain a positive mental perspective by reframing our situation. That is, we can have a key "go-to" thought that triggers our mindset in a new, more positive direction.

Several years ago I was working with a particular couple toward reconciliation. One day I happened to be meeting with the husband alone. All of a sudden, he began to describe in vivid detail an event that happened between him and his wife. Because of the striking freshness of his story, I figured the event must have happened recently. So I asked him where they were that weekend when the event had taken place. To this he replied, "Oh no, this happened *seven years ago.*" It was obvious that there was no reconciliation regarding the event and that he was still stewing over it in his heart and mind, even after seven years.

If you repeatedly throw a past offense in your spouse's face, incessantly gossiping to others about it and negatively dwelling on the situation in your mind, it is like having a scab on your arm that you keep ripping off. The wound in your soul is trying to heal, but every time you *think* and *talk* about it, you pick the scab off and begin bleeding all over again.

If this seems to describe what you are going through, I encourage you to leave it alone. Follow God's command and over time, make the choice to forgive. Seek a new course of action. Post some healthy signs inside your heart—no fishing, no talking, and no trespassing. Invite God into your life and your relationship and ask Him to do what only He can do—heal you from the inside out.

STEP 4

CHANGE

The final step of reconciliation is *change*. The necessity of change actually goes back to true repentance. The original Greek word for repentance is *metanoia*, and it means "a change of mind, to turn away from, or move in another direction."[2] To truly repent indicates that we are making a concerted effort to *be* and *do* something different. One description I have heard regarding repentance that I like is: *repentance is a radical rearrangement of life.* A lack of change makes the offended party wonder if we really are sorry for what we did. You and I can't keep doing the same things over and over again and expect different results. That is defined as insanity.

In order to truly change we must repent, and repentance starts with God. If we have wronged our spouse, we must first go to God and say something like, "Lord, I am sorry for what I have done (name the offense specifically). Please forgive me. What I did was wrong, and I don't want to keep doing it. I want to change my thinking and actions, but I cannot do it in my own strength. Help me, please. Give me Your strength to live differently. In Your Name, amen!" Then you go to your spouse, sincerely apologize, and ask for his or her forgiveness.

Now you have initiated change! The air is clear between you and your spouse, and your heart and mind are open and pointed toward your power Source—God Himself. And "He gives power to the faint and weary, and to him who has no might He increases strength [causing it to multiply and making it to abound]" (Isaiah 40:29 AMP).

True repentance produces change—a turning away from wrong thinking and behavior toward a new way of living.

REVISITING SAMANTHA AND PETE

A Picture of True Reconciliation

To give you a clear example of what the process of reconciliation looks like, let's turn our attention back to the couple in the restaurant, Pete and Samantha. The offense has already been committed. Now listen as they work toward reconciliation.

"Pete, when you made that joke about me at the restaurant," Samantha begins, "everyone laughed at me, and I felt humiliated and deeply hurt. I also felt betrayed. You're my husband, Pete, and we're supposed to support and protect one another. With everything in me, I held back the tears, but the situation was really awkward for me."

With a deep sigh of regret, Pete replies, "You know, Samantha, you're right. I did put you down and make fun of you in front of our friends. I can see how you would feel hurt and humiliated by my actions and how you would feel betrayed. I am so sorry."

As tears well up in Pete's eyes, he continues. "I really should be building you up in front of others, not tearing you down. If you want, I will go back to our friends, apologize for my actions, and tell them I was wrong."

"No, that's okay," Samantha responds with relief in her voice. "I can see that you're sorry for what you did and you understand where I'm coming from."

Reaching his hand toward hers, Pete asks, "Will you forgive me?"

"Yes, I forgive you," she replies gently. "And I will do my best to not keep bringing up the incident or dwelling on my negative emotions about it."

This is a picture of true reconciliation. While it doesn't always follow this exact pattern, it should be a simple process. Admitting our faults and confessing our wrongs is godly and opens the door to healing and restoration. God's Word says,

> *Therefore confess your sins to each other and pray for each other so that you may be healed. The prayer of a righteous man is powerful and effective.*

> **—JAMES 5:16**

Pete and Samantha dealt with the issue, restored peace in their marriage, and moved on. As you and your spouse engage in this process, you will preserve your emotional connection, prevent bitterness and resentment from creeping into your marriage, and build your House of Intimacy. While the consequences of failing to reconcile are far-reaching, the payoffs for pursuing and making peace are well worth it.

Admitting our faults and confessing our wrongs is
godly and opens the door to healing and restoration.

WHAT'S STOPPING YOU?

What makes reconciliation so difficult? Why are we so hesitant and reluctant to make peace with our spouse and others? I find that there are at least two reasons. They are both heart issues that we all need to continue working to overcome. The first is *pride* and the second is *fear.*

Pride says, "I don't want to admit my faults or own up to my wrongdoing." We can be so stubborn and bullheaded sometimes, can't we? *I'm not the one that's wrong,* we think to ourselves. *It's my husband/wife's fault. They're to blame for this ridiculous situation, not me.*

Fear is also a hindrance to reconciliation. We are afraid to confess our wrongs to others, because it would mean that we'd take a hit on our sense of value and worth. *My self-image is too fragile,* we often unconsciously think. *I just can't handle the potential rejection of being wrong or at fault for something.*

I believe that both pride and fear are forms of self-protection. Rather than being concerned with God's glory and the wellbeing of the person we have offended, we are focused on our own ego and self-preservation. In a sense, we are looking to protect our needs for value and security that were addressed in chapters 2 and 3.

I know that this was (and sometimes still is) the case for me. When I used to avoid conflict, got defensive, or minimized issues, I was motivated by the need to protect my sense of value and worth. I had a deep need to be "perfect." Thankfully, as God has worked in my life and I have come to find my sense of value and worth in Him, I have been freed to admit my faults and engage with my wife and others in making peace. I have found that it is much more liberating to simply admit my faults, deal with them, and move on, than it is to live in a world ridden with self-protection and self-preservation.

So stop and think: *What is keeping me from admitting my faults and pursuing peace?* I encourage you to search your heart and deal with any skeletons that may be in your closet. It is senseless to avoid conflict, blame others, and live in a world of self-protection. This only serves to cause further hurt, pain, and relational friction. I strongly encourage you to get engaged in the process of reconciliation. You will be so glad you did!

Chapter Summary 11

Reconciliation is a four-step process that includes repentance, forgiveness, getting our heart out on the table, and change. We get our heart out on the table by openly sharing our true thoughts and feelings with our spouse. We repent by having genuine sorrow for the offense we've caused and accepting responsibility for our actions. This leads to asking for or extending forgiveness, depending on which side of the offense we are on. True repentance will produce change—a turning away from wrong thinking and behavior toward a new way of living.

(1) Richard Exley, *Life's Bottom Line—Building Relationships That Last* (Tulsa, OK: Honor Books, 1990, p. 267). (2) Adapted from *Thayer's Greek-English Lexicon of the New Testament*, Joseph H. Thayer (Grand Rapids, MI: Baker Book House Company, 1977, p. 405).

Making It Yours ─────────────────────────────────

1. Overall, how is this chapter on reconciliation encouraging and motivating you to engage in the process of reconciliation with your spouse? What new perspectives are you seeing regarding the process of working through and resolving conflicts?

   _____

   _____

   _____

2. Of the four steps to reconciliation—*getting your heart out on the table, repenting, forgiving,* and *changing*—which seems to be the most challenging to you in your marriage? Why do you think this is the case?

   _____

   _____

   _____

3. Are there any barriers or obstacles currently between you and your spouse? If so, what are they? Are you willing to humble yourself and work toward a peaceful solution(s)? Pause and pray: "Lord, what's *my part* in this situation? What can *I* do to help promote reconciliation and restore peace between me and my husband/wife?" Listen and write down anything you feel the Lord is prompting you to do.
   The OBSTACLES my spouse and I are currently facing are...

   _____

   _____

   _____

I believe God is showing me that MY PART in helping to promote reconciliation is...

_____

_____

_____

_____

4. In light of the obstacles you mentioned, if there was one thing deep in your heart that you would like to share with your spouse—some aspect of your true thoughts and feelings—what would it be? If you knew they would listen to you and calmly, humbly receive your words, what would you say?

_____

_____

_____

_____

5. If you are finding it hard to forgive, think about this. What are some of the things you have done throughout your lifetime that you needed forgiveness for—from God and your spouse? How would your life be different if one day when you had repented and asked God to forgive you that He said, "No, you've hurt Me too many times. I can't forgive you." Carefully read God's promise to you in 1 John 1:9 and Jesus' words in Matthew 6:14-15. How do these verses motivate you to extend forgiveness to your spouse and others?

_____

_____

_____

_____

"The manna of one day was corrupt when the next day came. I must every day have fresh grace from heaven, and I obtain it only in direct waiting upon God Himself. Begin each day by tarrying before God, and letting Him touch you."

—ANDREW MURRAY[1]

CHAPTER 12

COMMITMENT AND GRACE: THE RECIPE FOR LONGEVITY

*Therefore, as God's chosen people, holy and dearly
loved, clothe yourselves with compassion, kindness,
humility, gentleness and patience. Bear with each other
and forgive whatever grievances you may have against
one another. Forgive as the Lord forgave you. And
over all these virtues put on love, which binds them all
together in perfect unity.*

—COLOSSIANS 3:12-14

WHEN I WORK with premarital couples, I often ask them this question: "What are your greatest fears and concerns regarding marriage?" With regularity, one of the typical answers I get is in the form of this question: "What if the flame in our marriage dies out?" In essence, they are concerned that their love for one another will grow cold or that they may lose interest in each other.

Sadly, the fire of romance being extinguished does seem to be a major cause of breakups today. Countless marriages end up in divorce, and the explanation often given is that they simply "grew apart" or "fell out of love." Thankfully, there are ways to protect against this.

That being said, when I meet with couples that are contemplating divorce, I ask them for the details of what is going on in their marriage and why they feel the need to divorce. After hearing each partner's story, I may respond with, "So you want to divorce over a 'for-better-or-for-worse' situation."

When you get right down to it, many marriages end over this kind of issue. Instead of choosing to fight *for* their marriage and do the hard work needed to save it, many couples simply choose a flight response of walking away from the conflict that exists. If this is where you find yourself—thinking about throwing in the towel and calling it quits—I urge you to reconsider. There is a better way—a way that leads to healing and restoration. It is through the grace of God.

How Valuable Are Your Vows?

When we as couples get married, we typically recite wedding vows to one another during the ceremony. One particular vow is a promise we make to our spouse before all who are present and, most importantly, before God—the One who ultimately officiates the wedding. In turn, we each recite this vow, first the man and then the woman, as we unite in marriage. It goes something like this:

"I, _____ (insert name), take you _____ (insert spouse-to-be's name), to have and to hold from this day forward, for better or for worse, for richer or for poorer, in sickness and in health, to love and to cherish, till death do us part."

This vow is a lifelong promise declaring that we are signing up to be committed to our spouse through thick and thin. We are pledging to navigate and get through all the ups and downs life hands us—together.

The "for better or for worse" part of the vow is a broad category that covers a lot of issues. Unfortunately, for many this vow goes by the wayside when we begin to face the challenges of marriage and don't like what we are experiencing. It's at this point that our vows change from the pursuit of *mutual* happiness and fulfillment to the pursuit of *personal* happiness and fulfillment.

While I'm not minimizing the hurt, pain, and negative relational patterns that may take place in a marital relationship, I am saying that the choice to divorce is extremely detrimental—especially when it involves children. It is a decision that should not be taken lightly.

Don't walk away from your marriage because of conflict. Choose to fight for it and do the work needed to save it.

When I got married to my wife, DeAnn, I did not struggle with the fear that many of my premarital couples have. I wasn't worried about the flame of love dying in our marriage. This wasn't because I knew that she was the perfect woman for me or because I was certain she would perfectly meet my needs and complete me as a person. Neither was it because I knew that I would perfectly meet her needs and make her happy.

The reason I didn't worry about our relationship lasting was because I knew that I was making a vow before God to DeAnn and that marriage is not ultimately about a romantic flame forever burning until death do us part. I also understood that marriage is not just about me getting my needs met and being happy. Marriage is first and foremost a commitment to God—to honor Him with our life and remain faithful to what He wants us to be and do as a follower of Christ. Second, marriage is a commitment to the one we chose as our spouse—a commitment we take seriously. Marriage is two joining together as one in an atmosphere of commitment and grace.

What Is the Foundation of Your Marriage?

Here is a good question to ask yourself concerning marriage: *Is my marriage founded on commitment and grace, or is it founded on performance, expectations, and having my needs met?* One thing I find fascinating is that when we as couples first meet and are dating, we are typically focused on the other person. We go out of our way to serve one another, doing special things and maintaining a mindset of self-sacrifice (other-centeredness) in the relationship. We do everything we can to make the person we are pursuing feel special and important.

Then when we walk down the aisle, take our vows, put rings on our fingers, and are pronounced husband and wife, things begin to change. Our mentality unconsciously goes from "What can I do for you?" to "What are you going to do for me?" Instead of having the attitude of "It is my responsibility to love you and complete you as a person," we begin thinking, "It is your responsibility to love me and complete me as a person."

What causes quarrels and fights between husbands and wives? God pulls back the curtain and reveals the answer through the apostle James.

> *What causes fights and quarrels among you? Don't they come from your desires that battle within you? You want something but don't get it. You kill and covet, but you cannot have what you want. You quarrel and fight. You do not have, because you do not ask God. When you ask, you do not receive, because you ask with wrong motives, that you may spend what you get on your pleasures.*

—JAMES 4:1-3

The quarreling and fighting begins in marriage as we lose sight of God, our marital commitment, and our spouse. Typically quarrels and fights in marriage revolve around something we want that we are not getting. A good question to ask is, "What is it that I want that I am not getting that is the root of my frustration?" The more we struggle and strive to have our own needs met, the more frustrating and unfulfilling married life becomes.

So what does it mean to live in a marriage that is founded on commitment and grace? As I did in the previous chapter, let me begin by explaining what it is **not**.

Marriage is a commitment to God—to honor Him
with our life and remain faithful to what He wants us
to be and do as a follower of Christ.

LIVING BY COMMITMENT AND GRACE DOES NOT MEAN WE OVERLOOK SIN AND SWEEP IT UNDER THE RUG.

Never confronting one another for the wrongs we have committed is a recipe for disaster. This is exactly what "avoiders" want to do. They have a "live and let live" mentality. However, this is just the opposite of what we are to do. Jesus instructs us in Matthew 18:15-17 how to confront one another when we have been sinned against. The purpose of confrontation is reconciliation and restoration of the relationship. God wants us to be reconciled to Him and each other. Pursuing peace is priority as we discussed in Chapter 11.

LIVING BY COMMITMENT AND GRACE DOES NOT MEAN WE NEVER BRING UP OUR CONCERNS, FRUSTRATIONS OR HURTS.

Being silent and keeping our frustrations to ourselves so that we don't "stir the pot" only leads to more hurt, resentment, and bitterness. Bringing up issues is not the problem. Avoiding or mishandling them is. Adequately dealing with our issues and maintaining peace is actually the solution.

As you and your spouse handle your frustrations and differences, keep in mind the principle of Romans 14:19. It instructs us to, "...make every effort to do what leads to peace and to mutual edification." So don't stuff your true thoughts and feelings. Simply ask God for His grace to speak the truth in love to your spouse in a way that will build them up in the midst of your differences, not tear them down.

LIVING BY COMMITMENT AND GRACE DOES NOT MEAN WE TOLERATE UNGODLY, DESTRUCTIVE BEHAVIOR.

If you are married to someone and they are engaging in extramarital affairs, physically abusive behavior, or acting in damaging and self-destructive ways such as drug or alcohol abuse, you are not to simply sit back and accept it. These types of situations require confrontation and demand action.

Confronting a spouse who is involved in these kinds of behavior is actually the gracious and loving thing to do. It can literally save your marriage and possibly your spouse's life. If you are in a situation of this nature, seek wise counsel and pray for your spouse to have a spirit of humility and repentance and a desire to work on overcoming their issues.

LIVING BY COMMITMENT AND GRACE DOES NOT MEAN WE HAVE NO EXPECTATIONS OF EACH OTHER.

Unconditional love doesn't mean we simply accept each other "as is" with no expectations of personal responsibility or growth. Having a desire or an expectation to see our spouse change for the better is not wrong. The real issue is how we handle our desires and expectations and how we treat one another in the process of waiting for positive improvement.

I encourage you to take your expectations and desires for your spouse and see how they measure up to these two questions:

First, is your expectation valid and realistic? And second, are you being compassionate, patient, and kind in the midst of your valid expectations? While our desire for change may often be valid, I have witnessed more often than not a need for more patience and compassion.

Again I ask the question: what does it mean to live in a marriage that is founded on commitment and grace?

Living by commitment and grace does not mean we overlook our spouse's wrongs, never bring up our concerns, or tolerate ungodly behavior.

LIVING IN A MARRIAGE FOUNDED ON COMMITMENT AND GRACE IS ONE IN WHICH...

EACH SPOUSE IS COMMITTED TO GOD AND BRINGING HIM GLORY.

Our marriage and life must be surrendered to God, first and foremost. As husbands and wives we mutually understand that marriage is not ultimately about our personal fulfillment, happiness, and contentment. It is about walking together with God and living out the Greatest Commandment, which is to "Love the Lord your God with all your heart and with all your soul and with all your mind, and to love your neighbor (which includes your spouse) as yourself" (see Matthew 22:37-39).

As I read the account of the life of Abraham in the book of Genesis, I cannot imagine him waking up one morning, going to his wife Sarah and saying, "You know Sarah, I feel like we're growing apart. There are things about you that I didn't fully realize when we got married. I feel like I just don't love you anymore. I need something different. I just can't see spending the rest of my life living this way. I am considering divorcing you and moving on to someone better." Why did Abraham not do such a thing? It is because his life's focus was on God. Honoring and walking with God was everything to him, and he and Sarah reaped the rewards of that focus.

EACH SPOUSE RECOGNIZES WE ARE ALL BROKEN.

As individuals living in a fallen world, none of us and none of our marriages will be perfect on this side of heaven. Life is broken by sin, and we will contend with its brokenness until God calls us home. I am a firm believer that there are no "haves" and "have-nots" in life. In reality, we are all "have nots" who daily live by the acceptance and grace of God through our Lord, Jesus Christ. We are all in the ongoing process of sanctification whereby we are being made more and more like Christ day by day. This is God's ultimate purpose for our life as believers.

A passage I love that conveys the idea that we are all in the same boat is Psalm 14:2-3. It states, "The Lord looks down from heaven on the sons of men to see if there are any who understand, any who seek God. All have turned aside, they have together become corrupt; there is no one who does good, not even one."

What these verses convey is that none of us completely love God and serve Him with a pure heart. All of us are prone to seek our own agenda and serve our own interests. We are like sheep that often go astray (see Isaiah 53:6). In other words, we are all in the same broken boat. There is no one who is perfect, not one. I believe this is how both husbands and wives need to approach their marriage, their lives, and resolving their marital issues.

As husbands and wives, we need to approach marriage realizing we are all broken and in need of God's grace.

EACH SPOUSE EXERCISES LOVE AND RESPECT.

As we navigate the daily issues life brings and we work together on resolving our frustrations, differences, and hurts, we are to be considerate of one another. This attitude of mutual love that is centered on commitment and grace is reflected in I Corinthians 13:4-7, which reads:

> *Love is patient, love is kind. It does not envy, it does not boast, it is not proud. It is not rude, it is not self-seeking, it is not easily angered, it keeps no record of wrongs. Love does not delight in evil but rejoices with the truth. It always protects, always trusts, always hopes, always perseveres.*

This kind of love is built on a firm, inner foundation of spiritual maturity, which grows from our personal relationship with Jesus Christ (see 1 John 4:7-21). It is not humanly possible to continually live in a state of patience, kindness, and humility toward others, particularly when they are challenging to live with. As we seek God and live in relationship with Him, He will empower us to overcome the tendencies to become impatient, envious, prideful, and self-seeking—all of which lead to marital break-down. With His strength, we can avoid looking to our own interests and focus on the interests of our spouse.

EACH SPOUSE EXAMINES THEMSELVES FIRST WHEN CONFLICTS ARISE.

Inevitably, disagreements are going to happen. One mark of a marriage founded on commitment and grace is not pointing a finger of blame at our mate the moment we run into a roadblock. Instead, we look at ourselves *first* to see what part we may have played in the dispute. Jesus makes this principle clear, stating:

> *"Why do you look at the speck of sawdust in your*
> *brother's eye and pay no attention to the plank in*
> *your own eye? How can you say to your brother,*
> *'Brother, let me take the speck out of your eye,' when*
> *you yourself fail to see the plank in your own eye? You*
> *hypocrite, first take the plank out of your eye, and*
> *then you will see clearly to remove the speck from your*
> *brother's eye."*

LUKE 6:41-42

Through all my years of counseling, it is extremely rare for a spouse to come into my office and say, "I know that I'm the problem in our marriage. I'm the one who is causing most of the issues. I'm the one that needs to change. So, I am here to work on me!"

It is just as rare to have a spouse begin by telling me all the wrong ways they have acted. That is, they don't go into detail of how they have hurt their spouse through their specific words and actions. On the contrary, what I normally get is a long story of how they feel they have been wronged in the marriage. "Oh, you just don't know how badly my spouse has mistreated me," they groan. They then explain how their spouse is responsible for over 90 percent of the problems in their relationship.

These words from the lips of Jesus in Luke 6 encourage us to be willing to spend more time looking at ourselves as we deal with issues in our marriage before we attempt to point out issues in our spouse. The old saying is true: when you point a finger of fault at someone else, there are three fingers pointing back at you. So be slow to cast blame.

As we seek God and abide in relationship with Him,
He will empower us to overcome the selfish tendencies
that lead to marital breakdown.

EACH SPOUSE TAKES THE COVENANT OF MARRIAGE SERIOUSLY.

The term *covenant* conveys the meaning of a contract, treaty, or promise. In essence, a covenant is "a binding agreement we make with another party or individual."[2] Interestingly, Jesus establishes that marriage is a covenant relationship when He responds to the Pharisee's question of whether it is permissible to divorce one's spouse for any reason. He says,

"Haven't you read," he replied, "that at the beginning
the Creator 'made them male and female,' and said,

212

*'For this reason a man will leave his father and mother
and be united to his wife, and the two will become one
flesh'? So, they are no longer two, but one. Therefore
what God has joined together, let man not separate."*

MATTHEW 19:4-6

Although the Bible does give valid grounds for divorce, the
grounds are very narrow and certainly not for any and every
reason (see Matthew 5:31-32). Biblically speaking, our marital covenant is an earthly representation of the covenant
God makes with us as believers in Christ. When He makes
a covenant with His people, it is established to be an eternal
relationship.

Imagine if God were to treat us as we often treat one another
in relationships and marriage. Picture Him coming to us one
day and saying, "You know, you keep failing Me as a follower
of Christ. I am tired of forgiving you for the same old stuff day
after day. I don't think I want you in My family anymore. I am
breaking My covenant relationship with you and casting you out
of My kingdom." How would we react? I think we would most
likely be beside ourselves with self-justification, fear and sorrow.
Thankfully, this is *not* the way God treats us. He honors His covenant, and He desires that we do the same with our earthly covenant of marriage.

AIM FOR EXCELLENCE...
NOT PERFECTION

As I close this book, I would like to reiterate that there is no "perfect" marriage. We are all fallen people living in a fallen world,
and nothing here on earth will be perfect this side of heaven. So,

if you are expecting perfection, you will be forever disappointed in what you have. This is exactly why living in a marriage that is founded on the above principles of commitment and grace is so imperative. If you continue to live in a marriage that is based on unrealistic expectations, the performance of your spouse, and simply having your needs met, you will live in a world of dissatisfaction and lack relational contentment.

"Well, Dave," you might ask, "What am I to shoot for? I've got to shoot for something." That is true. As the adage goes, if we aim for nothing we will hit it every time. I encourage you to *aim for excellence.* Whether you are trying to overcome major challenges, escape stagnation, or simply working to build a better marriage, your situation can greatly improve! All that is needed is for you and your spouse to be willing to take a serious look at yourselves, understand your own contributions to the breakdown in your marriage, and do the needed work to begin making relational improvements. I am a firm believer that your *House of Intimacy* may be rekindled if you are willing to seriously work at rebuilding it from the ground up, starting with the foundation of companionship and fostering a true partnership. This foundation paves the way for the rest of the house.

My prayer, now that you have read this book, is that you have a better understanding of the dynamics of *what* is going on in your marriage—*why* you are experiencing what you are experiencing. And most importantly, you also have the tools on *how* make significant strides forward. May God grant you His grace and blessing as you endeavor to move ahead for the sake of your marriage, your family (if you have children), and His glory. Amen!

CHAPTER SUMMARY 12

Marriage is a commitment to honor God with our life and remain faithful to what He wants us to be and do as a follower of Christ. It is also a serious commitment to the one we have chosen as our spouse. Our commitment is lived out through God's grace. We honor Him and bring Him glory. We recognize there is no perfect marriage and we are all broken. We receive His grace and extend grace to our spouse. As we abide in relationship with Him, He empowers us to overcome the selfish tendencies that lead to marital breakdown.

(1) Christian Quotes on the *Grace of God* (http://www.dailychristianquote.com/page/10/?s=grace+of+god, accessed 3/22/16). (2) Adapted from the *Definition of Covenant* (http://www.merriam-webster.com/dictionary/covenant, accessed 3/18/16).

Making It Yours ———————————————————————

1. A healthy marriage is one that is built on **commitment** and **grace**. Stop and take a good look at your relationship. Ask yourself, *Is my marriage founded on commitment and grace? Or is it founded on performance, expectations, and having my needs met? How valuable are the vows I spoke to my spouse on our wedding day? Am I still honoring my commitment to God and my mate?* With God's help, answer as honestly as you can.

———————————————————————————————————

———————————————————————————————————

———————————————————————————————————

———————————————————————————————————

2. In light of your answers to question 1, what needs to change in *you*? How can you better honor your commitment to God and your spouse *from your heart* instead of it being mere formality or lip service? In what practical ways can you "fan the flame" and rekindle a fresh fire of love in your relationship? **I believe the things that need to change in *me* are...**

———————————————————————————————————

———————————————————————————————————

I can better honor my commitment to God and my spouse from my heart by...

———————————————————————————————————

———————————————————————————————————

Some practical ways I can rekindle a fresh fire of love include...

———————————————————————————————————

———————————————————————————————————

———————————————————————————————————

3. The key to working through all the challenges that marriage and life bring and enjoying a healthy relationship is God's *grace.* His grace is His strength and ability to do what we could never do on our own. God has a lot to say about grace in His Word. Carefully read these verses and jot down what He is showing you about His grace. How can you apply this in your life and marriage?

    The Source of Grace – John 1:16; 2 Corinthians 9:8; Philippians 1:7

    _____

    _____

    _____

    Recieving Grace – Romans 5:2; Hebrews 4:15-16; James 4:6

    _____

    _____

4. Undoubtedly, there is probably an area of your life where you really need grace from God and your spouse to grow. What area(s) might that be and what might "receiving" grace look like? How about for your spouse? In what area(s) of his or her life do they need grace most? What might "giving" grace to them look like (in a practical sense)?

    The areas of MY life where I really need grace from God and my spouse are...

    _____

    _____

    _____

    In a practical sense, RECEIVING GRACE from my spouse in these areas might look like...

    _____

    _____

    _____

The area(s) of my SPOUSE'S life where they really need grace are...

_____

_____

_____

In a practical sense, GIVING GRACE to my spouse in these areas might look like...

_____

_____

_____

ABOUT THE AUTHOR

DAVE HOLDEN IS an author, speaker, and Licensed Professional Counselor (LPC). He is the co-founder of Genesis Christian Counseling in St. Louis, Missouri and holds a Master of Divinity ('95) and Master of Arts in Counseling ('96) from Covenant Theological Seminary. Dave completed his undergraduate degree in Business Administration ('84) from Gordon College in Wenham, Massachusetts. He also has extensive training in biblical peacemaking and performs mediation services for marriages, families, churches, and ministries in conflict.

Since 1996, Dave has specialized in marriage and family therapy. He also works particularly with those dealing with depression, anxiety, anger, and addictions, as well as spiritual, identity, and life-transition issues. Additionally, Dave is dedicated to working with pastors and ministry leaders who are experiencing stress, burnout, and other ministry-related issues. One of his gifts and passions is to help individuals gain life-changing insights to their situations through God's timeless and relevant Word, considering their life from a fresh perspective.

Dave has developed many classes on biblically-based topics, such as contentment, marriage, cultivating the fruit of the Spirit, and biblical peacemaking. He has also created a Premarital Counseling Program and does extensive work in helping couples get a solid start in their relationship.

Contact Dave at…
Genesis Christian Counseling, LLC
2190 S. Mason Road, Suite 306
St. Louis, MO 63131

dholden.genesis@gmail.com
www.genesischristaincounseling.org

52622455R00130

Made in the USA
Columbia, SC
08 March 2019